Alight Within

THE HANDBOOK FOR THE LIGHTBRINGER ESSENCES

by Rachel Singleton

AN ASH KEYS PUBLICATION

Alight Within

The Handbook For The LightBringer Essences

by Rachel Singleton
Founder of the LightBringer Essences

Edited by John Williams
Photographs by Bryan and Rachel Singleton
Illustration/cosmogram by Salvatore Cali
Designed and set by Jackie Stewart and Rachel Singleton

First published by Ash Keys Publishing
2, Little Langdale,
AMBLESIDE. LA22 9NT. UK.

A catalogue record for this book is available from the British Library.

This book is dedicated to Margaret Hall
with love and deep thanks

CONTENTS

Preface

As is the case for so many people, some of the first flower essences I ever used were those of Dr Bach's Rescue Remedy combination and the Australian Bush 'Emergency Essence'. It is uncanny how essences seem to call us when we are at a desperate place and have nothing else to turn to. With time, this does not have to be the case, but it is often the portal through which we pass in order to enter this world.

As a newly qualified secondary school English teacher, I was going through a period of ill-health brought on by daily stress and mounting exhaustion. Incipient stomach problems I'd had through my teens had become more acute and turned into full blown Irritable Bowel Syndrome which was incredibly debilitating, leading me to become malnourished though my appetite was good, simply because I wasn't absorbing the nutrients properly from my food. I was experiencing regular migraines, looked as pasty-faced as it was possible to be, had lost the noble art of falling asleep and staying that way for the night (though I could sleep for England during the day), and was suffering from all sorts of other minor niggles which came from nowhere and are now thankfully falling back into the oblivion of distant memory.

I discovered that none of this was something conventional medicine could help with, though blood was taken on a fairly regular basis and I was tested for everything under the sun. The results always came back as 'normal'. Medically I was apparently within the realms of health. In reality I was most definitely not. I vaguely comprehended that the solution needed to be internal and that anything that was, in effect, administering sticking plaster externally would not take me forward in myself as a person or in my health; however, alternative therapies had until this point been outside the radar of my experience. It was a timely suggestion from my husband to think outside the box and try something different which led us to select a homeopathic remedy one day, whilst on a camping trip in the wilds of Scotland. Each night, once the cold of the evening set in, I would feel acute spasms in my intestinal area and become doubled up in pain. The first remedy I tried eased the symptoms a little; but they then returned and it refused to work again. The second remedy I tried took my breath away with its efficacy – the pain dissolved from my being within minutes. It was the sweetest, most gentle feeling. I felt myself relax deliciously into the absence of pain.

On returning to England, I signed up to see a homeopath. Here I received homeopathy *and* flower essences and began to make significant progress, realising how profoundly linked was my physical state with unresolved emotions I still carried from earlier times in my life. But it was not until I embarked on a professional training as a homeopath in the Autumn of that year that I found the tools which would take me forward – the need to examine compassionately and process gently one's emotions; an understanding of subtle energy and how energy moves and/or becomes stuck in our meridians, chakras and physical body; and the importance of diet. And here, above all, I learnt what a flower essence really is . . . and thus discovered a connection that struck my soul with the most profound recognition, relief and delight.

I had the good fortune to be taught by Beth Tyers, now sadly deceased. Beth Tyers was one of the foremost teachers on essences in the UK, profoundly tuned in to the Australian Bush, Bailey and later the Indigo and Alaskan essences in particular, but with an innate comprehension of essences as a whole which she was able to impart joyfully, convincingly, practically and personally.

I remember the first time I was taught by Beth, which took place during my homeopathic training. That afternoon Beth arrived with a huge and glorious bunch of flowers – an image which stays with me now. Listening to her description of the healing gifts of flowers, hearing of her own journey, and then – joy of joys! – being able to attune to flowers and flower essence cards to select what we needed to help ourselves at that time, was a most beautiful experience. It was an afternoon which changed my world. As she went round each of us and told us about the essences we had selected, it was like being in the presence of a seer and having one's soul disclosed to one, through the soft textures and gentle colours of the world of flowers. I felt a recognition thrill through me that was both spiritual and visceral and I felt incredibly alive, impatient and ready to begin. I knew in that moment that I wanted to work with flower essences, take flower essences, breathe in flower essences and above all – make flower essences. With Beth's gentle guidance in those early days, and the support of other gifted teachers and producers since, I have been able to take that journey, and it seems that each step along the way has organically and sweetly unfolded before me.

At that time, there were few female producers of essences in this country and many of the wild plants that I knew and loved in Cumbria, and in Scottish moors, bogs and pine forests, had not been made into essences. I wanted to bring forth their exquisite quality, their wild grace and their healing; to offer a range of essences which would touch and tend the feminine energy in us; to use only plants, gems and locations that were wild and pristine; and to create a range which felt whole and would suit practitioner and lay-person alike. As time has gone on, it has been the more rare and unusual flowers of the British Isles (and beyond) that I have been drawn to. And through these I have learnt to make essences in a way which is more wholistic and organic, that freed me from having to pick and harm the plant, and which gives us essences which harness the living energy of the plant and are truly sustainable.

Flower essences are a healing craft for which I feel the deepest reverence. The LightBringer Essences are the result of over a decade of returning to a deep listening to Spirit-in-Self, heeding the call that comes from the flowers, and trustingly placing one step in front of the other.

Here, I offer to you with love, the knowledge, experience, journey and above all essences that are the result of my path so far. I invite you to question, explore and try out for yourself for I can only speak the nature of reality as I have found it and the knowledge that has worked for me. There are no absolutes, but it is my hope that you will find accord in these pages and perhaps some enduring blooms of understanding and healing that provide sustenance for you on your path.

May your journey be beautiful!

Foreword

When I first came across the writings of the flower essence pioneer Edward Bach many years ago, I felt a thrill of recognition as something inside me knew with absolute certainty there was a beautiful truth being revealed to me. A similar feeling engulfed me on reading *Alight Within*.

The essences that Dr. Bach was inspired to make were a reflection of his own life journey, his individual sensitivity, as well as the spirit of the times in which he lived and worked. And I think the same can be said for all of the essence ranges that have been developed by other pioneers around the world. Consequently, if you really want to get to know a range of essences, it helps to have some familiarity with the person who has brought them into being, as the two are inextricably linked.

Rachel Singleton has put so much of herself - literally, her heart and soul - into creating this beautiful range of essences. As you take the time to read and savour the introductory chapters you will get to know both the LightBringer Essences and their founder in a deeper and more intimate way. Rachel reminds us - and it is a timely reminder - that there is so much more to making and taking essences than you would ever guess from their physical appearance in those little dropper bottles.

Rachel describes from her own hard-earned experience what these essences - and perhaps all essences - are really about. Reading these pages will help you to understand the level that essences are actually working on, and how best to attune yourself to that level so that you can, through your work with them, refine your sensitivity and skill as a healer and an essence prescriber.

The LightBringer Essences, more than any others I have come across, unite the opposite energies of roaring, elemental wildness with the most exquisitely tender gentleness. They do not shy away from the painful and difficult places within, yet they reach out towards the light that embraces the very depths of darkness.

Addressing accurately so many of the concerns of modern life, you will find a deep resonance in the essence descriptions with your own struggles, and, if you are a practitioner, with the life challenges faced by your clients. I have found the LightBringers to be particularly helpful as transformational agents in the area of personal relationships, that crucible within which so many opportunities for healing and growth are to be found.

If you are new to the world of essences, this book will open your heart and mind to the wonderful healing potentialities that they hold. And if you are already familiar with essences, *Alight Within* will refresh and inspire you to deepen your understanding and expand your capacity as a healer and as a human being.

Ian Watson, May 2010.

How To Use This Book

Part One of this book is written with the intention of providing an in-depth understanding of how to work with the LightBringer Essences, and how to understand their uses and the responses we can have to them.

Part Two shows certain key areas that can be supported by the essences and assists you to compare and differentiate between them. This section helps to illuminate how the essences feel and look under different circumstances, and offers some insights into how they may be practically applied and the depths they can touch.

Part Three is the 'materia medica' of the book - the full detailed description of each essence given in alphabetical order. Included in this section are the key notes, indications for use and energetic applications for each one, as well as the image and affirmation (as found also on the Essence Cards). The energetic applications indicate the chakras and layers of the aura that a particular essence most resonates with and touches. These are based on the physicist and healer Barbara Ann Brennan's descriptions of the chakras and the different layers of the human energy-body. Further reference for those who are not familiar with subtle energy anatomy and who wish to pursue this can be found in her book, *Hands of Light*. However, this information is not vital for most people to comprehend in order to work effectively with the essences. The individual essences are followed by detailed descriptions of each of the combinations, including a break-down of the essences found in each of these.

Part Four includes a comprehensive repertory which gives brief descriptions of relevant essences under themes such as Grief, Self-Realisation, Anger, etc. From this you can go directly to the particular area you need an essence to treat, and select those that are most pertinent.

The final **Appendix** contains Julian Barnard's summary of how Dr Bach originally made essences, reproduced by his kind permission from the book *The Healing Herbs of Edward Bach*. This will be of interest to anyone who is drawn to making essences themselves.

Quick Reference to Taking and Selecting Essences

The following pages give the basic instructions regarding how to **select essences**, how to **make a dosage bottle**, and how to **administer them in different ways**. In **Part One** these instructions are considered in more depth and in the context of the aims of essence work as a whole and I recommend you read **Part One** before progressing to use the essences so that you have a more comprehensive sense of how, why and when essences are selected and taken in particular ways. In this way you can begin to find your own individual way of working with the LightBringer Essences and of making them your own.

SELECTING ESSENCES

There are several ways of selecting essences. The process is a mindful one, best done in a quiet and peaceful space where you can set aside the time to focus on your specific healing needs. From here, seek to select the essence/essences which feel most supportive for you at this time (it is possible to combine up to 6 essences). You can select essences in three main ways: **repertory**, **intuitive**, or **knowledge-based**.

The **repertory** at the back of the book gives a comprehensive range of themed areas such as 'Grief and Loss', 'Oneness', 'Purification and Cleansing', followed by a list of the relevant essences and brief descriptions. If you are specifically looking for essences for a particular issue, then this is a fast and useful way of finding which essences cover this. You can pick out those whose descriptions are closest to your needs, read the more detailed Individual Essence description for verification and select from there.

You can also **select essences intuitively**. There are several ways of doing this. Selecting intuitively means using any method that allows you to bypass the more linear thought-based part of your mind and surrender to your deeper knowing and sensing. To select intuitively you need first to set your intent for healing by asking to be shown those essences that best fulfil your healing needs at this time. From here you can then proceed to use any one of the following methods:

1. Use a pendulum to dowse over the bottles, the Essence Cards, or a list of the essences.

2. Sit with the book in your hands and intuitively open it on a particular page.

3. If you have a set of the essences or cards, sit with these in front of you and, with your eyes closed, reach with your hand for the essences.

4. Scan the essence bottles or cards (face down) with your eyes open or closed, feeling for an energetic pull that draws you towards specific essences.

5. With the cards face up and your eyes open, go to those whose images you are particularly drawn to at this time (this can also be a wonderful method for children to use to select their own essences).

At all times during the intuitive selection process it is important to keep repeating your intent so that you stay deeply connected with your own or another's healing needs at this time.

A knowledge-based approach comes from working with the essences over time. As they become more and more familiar to you, you may well find yourself listening to someone and developing a sense that they need Alpine Willowherb for the sadness you can sense in their heart, Primrose for the poor boundaries they have in their relationships, and Golden Light for the lack of joy and hope they feel regarding their future. This hands-on knowledge comes surprisingly soon and you will find you become familiar with a core group of the essences very quickly and can then expand your knowledge from there.

MAKING A DOSAGE BOTTLE

LightBringer Essences come in **stock bottles**. These are 15ml bottles that consist of 60% organic brandy, 40% spring water from organic land and approximately 0.01% tincture of essence. The brandy preserves the essence, keeps it free from bacteria, and helps hold stable its energetic imprint. *For people who do not wish to take alcohol internally, please read on for alternative ways of administering essences.*

The essences can either be taken directly from the bottle or you can make up a dosage bottle containing several essences of your choice.

As a general rule, **stock concentrate** is particularly suitable for immediate use in acute situations, whilst a dilute strength **dosage bottle** of essences is usually for taking longer term, thereby enabling the essences to go in gently and work deeply over a period of time. Making a dosage bottle from your stock essences means the stock bottle will go further and, if you are taking several essences at once, you can simply carry one bottle around with you. It also enables you to give many different bottles of tailor-made combinations to other people, making essences highly economical to use.

Dosage Bottle: Using a 30ml (1 oz) bottle with dropper pipette (see mail order details at the back of the book), place 20% vodka or brandy in the bottle and 80% spring water. To this mix add 5 drops of each of the essences you wish to combine. A maximum of 6 essences is generally recommended. The alcohol will preserve the mixture and keep it free from germs for a period of about 6 weeks – more than sufficient for you to finish your bottle of essences. Take 5 drops morning and night. **Store in a cool dry place. Use within 6 weeks.**

ADMINISTERING THE ESSENCES

Essences are commonly taken orally - either straight from a stock or dosage bottle.

Taking essences orally: Place 5 drops on the tongue, being careful to avoid touching your mouth with the pipette in order to keep it clean. Take twice daily until you finish the bottle or, in an acute situation, place 5 drops of stock in a glass of water and sip until the situation that is causing you distress has abated.

It is also possible to use the essences in other ways:

- **Spray** - place 5 drops of stock in spring water in an unused misting bottle (available from our online shop or from chemists) and spray around yourself / the room. Store in the fridge for up to 4 weeks. Or use 30% vodka and 70% spring water for a longer-lasting spray. You may wish to add a couple of drops of a favourite essential oil to the spray to add another dimension.
- **Skin** - gently rub 2 or 3 drops into the temples, wrists, abdomen or where needed, or add to a water-based cream. Do not apply to open wounds.
- **Bath** - add 5 drops to the bath water (or 2 drops for a baby's bath).

- **Water** - add 5 drops to a cup of either hot water (to let the alcohol evaporate off) or cold; sip until finished. Add 5 drops to a drinking bottle of spring water or juice and take throughout the day by sipping as you need them.
- **For animals** - place 2 or 3 drops on your hands and rub through their fur, or use a spray and mist around their sleeping area (do not spray directly towards an animal).

RECOMMENDED DOSE

The recommended dose for LightBringer Essences is 5 drops two to three times daily.

In general it is the frequency of the dosage that is important, not how much is taken. If you take more than 5 drops at any one time then it only wastes the essences; it does not necessarily give you a 'bigger' dose.

In acute situations you may want to take the drops as **stock concentrate**, 3 to 4 times daily for a few days.

Longer term, taking the drops twice daily from a **dosage bottle** until it is finished gives them time and space to work, going slowly and deeply in to areas of your being where they are most needed.

Sometimes you may feel an initial intensification of your emotions or experiences when taking essences. This is not the case for everyone by any means and it does not happen very often for the majority of people. **Simply taking fewer drops of the essences and taking them less frequently will enable you to find the level that is most comfortable for you.**

Part One
Introduction to Essences

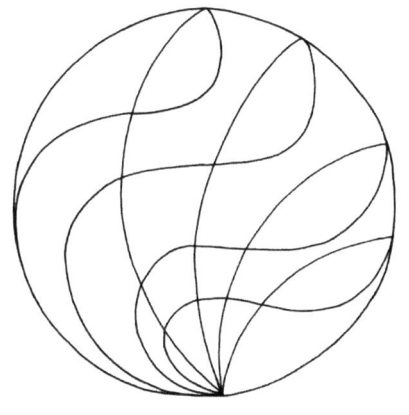

Making the LightBringer Essences: Heeding the Call

> In front of a huge old tree, her attention riveted to it, knelt a young girl of perhaps seven or eight years old. She had long golden hair and wore a dress and pinafore that looked Victorian. The scene contained nothing other than these two figures – the tree and the girl – and the soft meadow surrounding them. Between them a most extraordinary communication was taking place. Tracing the bark with her fingers, as if she were de-coding Braille, the girl read the tree; its fissures, knolls and striations imparting its essence to her as clearly and tangibly as words on a page. Perceiving through her eyes, I felt the palpable connection of wood and life-force and knew, with a sense of thrill and wonder, that the tree's wisdom, history, knowledge and very being were woven through the structure and fabric of its bark.

On waking from this dream in my late teens I was engulfed by a profound grief, for on waking I instantly knew that I had lost the gift of the dream; the effortless percipience with which I could directly read, commune with and learn from Nature. The experience felt as natural as breathing, deeply nourishing and humbling; the loss of it felt temporarily overwhelming. Ten years later I began to comprehend this dream and its sweet significance.

Introduced to essences through my homeopathic training (see **Preface**), I was instantly struck by their gentle grace and potential. For myself there was a deep personal recognition, a sense of coming home. I knew I had found what I wanted to do in my life. But perhaps more importantly I was struck by the beauty of this as a healing modality which truly embraced, sustained and upheld a person's true nature and healing path. Here is a therapy which harnesses the numinous quality of a plant – not its physical properties or chemical construct but its light-filled essence – in a way which we can take within in order to nurture and bring healing to our own essence. This is 'Soul Medicine'. It does not touch us on the level of the herbal, homeopathic, nutritional or pharmaceutical but directly resonates core to core, life-force to life-force, spirit to spirit; it resonates in the way it grows, the how and where, in its peculiar qualities, its individual expression and in the fulfilment of its own nature.

The flower of a plant is said to be the culmination of its being, biologically, aesthetically and metaphysically. It is the apex of its growth cycle, the means by which it goes on to reproduce; a source of attraction to insects, birds, animals and humans alike; and a rich source of symbolism and beauty for many cultures. Flowers touch us in the deepest ways. They are one of the most poignant and potent ways of acknowledging love, death, tragedy, celebration – helping us to express that which goes beyond words, enabling us to walk into areas of the psyche where mundane explanations and responses are simply inappropriate - where the radiance, intimacy, light and blossoming of flowers can intuitively speak for us.

Making an essence is a mindful, alchemical process, though the actual practical methodology of it appears surprisingly simple. Dr Bach's methodology (see **Appendix**) is the blueprint from which all subsequent essence ranges have been made. As the founder of modern-day flower essences, we owe much to his brave journey in searching beyond the acceptable parameters of allopathic medicine for something which would reach much more deeply than drugs removing or suppressing symptoms. As many before and since have realised, symptoms are the language through which the body communicates to us that there is something wrong, something inherently out of balance. It does not make sense therefore to eliminate the early warning system. Rather we need to understand its language, come to a deep and living perception of how this communicates within ourselves as a unique individual, and through this discourse learn how to restore and maintain our being in balance.

Taking an essence enables clearer communication to take place between our self and this inner knowing (our Higher Self / True Self / Spirit – however we wish to describe it). The drops we take within ourselves are the liquid imprint of the plant's own harmonious resonance, vitality and life-force. They are its consciousness, its spirit-in-matter released; literally – its essence. As this is imparted to us by taking the flower essence, this sets up a resonance with our own essential self, our harmonious and inherently spiritual nature. A connection is made, the way becomes clearer. This aspect of our being is nourished and illuminated, and thus we are able to hear its call more brightly and clearly. We begin to regain our insight, our sense of inner knowing, our connection with our own storehouse of wisdom and guidance. We begin to restore pathways within that are deeply insightful and healing, which may have been lost through experiences, teachings and the conformities that have overlaid them in everyday living. The internal detritus that accumulates when we live from a place that is set down by external authorities, without checking how this correlates with our own sense of what needs to be, begins to shift and dissolve. We begin to trace our way back through the debris to our own voice, consciousness and conscience. We find an inner balance point.

I see essences as the means by which the pathways back are illuminated, cleared, eased and made fluent. They light the way. They bring warmth, restore joy, rekindle light, restore our comfort and bring ease. They are a means for us to journey back to ourselves. And they keep the channels clear and the bright Self's path illuminated once we are back there.

FIRST STEPS

At the point when I first endeavoured to make essences, I knew only a little of this. I could grasp it intuitively but it was not formulated as fully-fledged thoughts and I did not yet have direct experience of this within my own life. Therefore I went first to my head to think through, plan and execute the making of my earliest attempts at essences. Following Dr Bach's guidelines, I created several essences. I had hit upon the notion of making individual essences of flowers of the same colour, that grew together or nearby, and which could then be combined to become a conglomerate essence for each of the chakras. There was nothing wrong with the idea but after making the first essences – daffodil, primrose and celandine I think – combining them, using them myself, giving them to willing friends and colleagues, I found that nothing was happening. There was absolutely no response.

I knew I had followed Bach's guidelines to the letter and couldn't understand why the resulting essences did not resonate for anyone. I had spent hours pouring over the plants' healing qualities in order to understand them and I felt I had made and combined them mindfully and sensitively. Discouraged and somewhat dismayed, I began to think that I had been wrong to assume that essences were the way forward for me and for a time I left off making them and continued with my training as a homeopathic practitioner.

Events in my own life took a bleak turn in 2000 however, and it was the darkness and severity of this time that eventually took me back to essence making. My beloved grandmother died after a prolonged and distressing decline over several months; my husband and I were witnesses to a fatal road accident; and I was myself suffering from bouts of intense and debilitating fatigue, poor health and depression. We had very little money, and lived in an isolated dark and damp house which had fungus growing out of the internal walls at an alarming rate. I was feeling utterly lost in myself, had very little work and was struggling to move forward. It was both a harrowing and stultifying time. It was as if nothing fresh, good or true was growing. Everything felt so dark.

However, the very events which seemed so hard (my grandmother's illness and death, the road accident, my ill-health) were to become in themselves extraordinary catalysts and the means by which I was propelled back towards something much lighter and – in time – more joyous. Because of the nature of my grandmother's waning, I felt that her death was a release for her after the three miserable months of decline she had suffered previously and so I experienced great sadness but also peace at her passing. I also felt surprisingly close to her, as if she were actually still around.

Two weeks after her funeral, I was having a very difficult day, lost in churning thoughts which were sad and quite despairing. The weather outside was beautiful. The sky was a deep and gorgeous blue, the sun warm, and the summer flowers were everywhere brightening the hedgerows and meadows. I walked down towards the river and as I came to its bank I was arrested by a diminutive white flower I saw growing there. It appeared to be everything I was not at that time and this realisation struck me instantly and with great force. The white star-like flowers were clear, distinct, pure, light and utterly defined. 'Angel Star' I thought and felt suddenly, palpably, as if Grandma was standing beside me. I did not know the name of the plant or anything about it but over the next few minutes two or three fully formed and complex sentences came into my mind which described the energetic qualities and healing of this plant. I began to understand that something was happening. Almost without thinking I gathered several stalks from the plant, held the flowers to my heart and set off walking home again, holding them there.

After some time, my dogs came racing back to me, wondering where on earth I had got to. I had been walking rapidly before, my thoughts racing, my whole being tense and knotted. Yet within seconds of taking those precious flowers to my breast, I felt a great stillness and settling within. I slowed down so much that I was barely walking. Everything that was not essentially 'me' washed away – all the worries, fears, aches, burdens, blind assumptions, despair. I felt more serene than I had ever felt in my life. I experienced being truly safe, calm, at one. I felt like me again and I felt both light and joyful. At this point, I think I began to understand the capacity of flowers to heal and still the troubles of heart and soul.

Taking the flowers back home, I placed them in a bowl in spring water and put them in the sunshine. I had arranged to visit a friend that day but could hardly bear to tear myself away from this precious process. Whilst I was with her however I was aware of feeling extraordinarily attuned, like a transmitter; I seemed to know things during our conversation that I would not normally know or have access too, things about her life which she had never disclosed to me, insights I could give about her situation now which she had barely described to me and which nevertheless felt incredibly pertinent to her. I felt as if I was burning from the sheer intensity of energy that was coming down through my core.

I returned home and after bottling the essence that bottle never left my side. I carried it everywhere, laid it down next to our bed at night, and held it at any time when I felt I needed its comfort. It seemed imbued with my grandma's loving presence, with the beauty of the flowers, with the sun, and with good, good things. I didn't take it at this point – I didn't need to – I just drank in its energy by being in its presence.

Eventually it dawned on me that I could make a stock bottle and actually take some of the essence. At the same time I felt I wanted to make up two or three bottles to share with some special people. One of them was my homeopath at the time; and after coming away from speaking to him about it, I felt my grandmother's hand on my shoulder as I drove back home, as clear and real as could be.

The following weeks brought many strange times. Some were the darkest I had known, but amongst them were some of the lightest. It was as if the dull grey that had shrouded me for months was being separated into stark experiences of dark and light. Being at the fatal road accident was harrowing and disturbing – yet holding the man's hand as he died, I found myself calm and completely sure as I prayed for him to be sent to the Light. It was the time after when we had to assimilate this and give our statements that we began to feel the horror of it. And subsequently it felt for weeks as if I saw 'the skull beneath the skin' in the face of everyone I met. Again, it was to flowers that I instinctively turned and found comfort.

I began to have days where every wild flower I looked at, I received information on. Information was streaming through me. I can only think that this was a time when the veil between life and death was very thin for me and I was walking between those two worlds. It was disturbing and yet exciting. I would burn with the intensity of this knowledge - it felt like hot currents of energy were coursing down the central axis of my body and words of understanding regarding a plant's essence were coming to me with incredible speed and ease. I experienced intense percipience, a profound sense of connection with nature and a more personal understanding of other people's pain.

THE CRUCIBLE

I understood very quickly that 'Angel Star' was the first of those beloved essences I had long since dreamed I would make. Over the coming months I lived the healing gifts of it. This was not an easy process – its teaching stems from its invitation to stay attuned to, heed, and walk forward with the message of one's inner knowing and teaching. Angel Star is like a thread of gold in a very dark maze – think of the story of the Minotaur. This empowers one to navigate through dark times, keeping hold of one's emerging truth and light, and in doing so it leads one to become aware of how people, circumstances and patterns pull you away from this. So there is the tension of one's own voice, alone in the darkness, and the needs and demands of life and other people! At that time in my life I faced this pattern everywhere I looked. I realised I had jettisoned my own self to keep the peace, and clawing this back was not generally accepted or welcomed by those closest to me, whom it most affected. Add to this that I was very naïve and defensive in the ways I did this and it was a painful and disturbing time.

But the essence and the growing awareness in me felt the same – like a gentle, warm and restorative light which kept me going. Like a lighthouse, something solid, immovable, and unchanging. I could not go back now I had seen the strings that held my previous way of being in place – but to go forward was intensely difficult, alien and lonely. I felt I was heading off on a trajectory which left everything familiar behind, where no one wanted to join me, where I risked pulling apart the fabric of everything I had. I felt poised – horribly – between destruction and freedom.

Colleagues and friends who were using Angel Star began to tell me things that were happening though, and these were like little rivulets of light coming in, confirming that the process was essentially good. My homeopathic friend told me of an elderly client who was on the point of committing suicide because life was so dark, lonely and unrewarding. The person would get to the brink of utter desolation and at times had attempted to end it all. My friend gave his client Angel Star and told me, 'This person keeps coming back now asking for more Angel Drops because whenever they feel they are approaching that place of darkness, they can take them and it brings them back. They said it's like choosing to turn round and come back to the light again.' Another friend said the bottle simply fell off the shelf above her desk whenever she needed to take it. One time she had been thinking she needed it, walked into her therapy room and saw it happen. She had absolutely no rational explanation for it. Another colleague said, 'It is so beautiful, so pure, so light. And yet it feels really strong and grounding. I find this the most gentle, reassuring thing.'

I wrote down all the feedback I got, collecting it like pearls for a necklace, finding my way to understanding more deeply what the essence touched and healed. Bringing together my various experiences - Grandma's slow, painful demise and the sense that she was with me in Spirit when I made this essence; the growing awareness of the clear defined self that yet shines brightly in dark times, as represented by the diminutive star flower; the sense of facing one's core issues, one's death, one's loneliness, one's mortality – all of these began to show me the extraordinary depth this essence, but also essences in general, can touch. My respect for essences deepened further at this time.

MAKING LIVING ESSENCES

It was not until another fourteen months had passed that I made the next essence. I experienced that 'Flower Essence Moment' – the quickening, the recognition from deep within, the flood of words and insight – on several occasions but felt it was not yet the right time to make the essences these flowers and experiences pertained to. Some took another four years before the place, time – and indeed me, the person making them – were all ready together. This is a theme which has continued since. Even now, 57 essences on, I cannot make an essence until I am ready. (There is one particular essence that is now six years into the process of not being made ...)

Grass of Parnassus was to become the second most important essence in terms of the development of the range and the future course they would take, and in terms of my own inner development. I had never noticed the plant until I began to notice flowers as essences, and then I could not believe I had missed it as it has to be one of our most lovely mountain flowers here in Britain. I went to the hills above my house to make this. Here there are two colonies of Grass of Parnassus. I chose the one that was in full sunlight early in the day and which had beside it a lovely old hawthorn with a low branch I could sit on. The day I went to make it was peaceful and sunny. I picked several of the blooms, releasing its delicate honey scent in doing so, and placed them in the bowls. I made the essence entirely according to Dr Bach's instructions, with the dew still heavy on them, at dawn, without touching them, and was myself dressed in unbleached, organic cotton clothing. I did not let my shadow cross the bowl. For two to three hours I waited with the essence in quiet meditation. It was a very powerful and lovely experience and during this process I had a clear visual image of what the essence was for:

> I saw myself standing with my aura full of holes. They were everywhere and they were dark as if there was an absence of anything there. Into these holes the flower heads of Grass of Parnassus were placed, plugging these holes. But they did not face outwards, they faced in towards me. They faced in and their gentle luminosity reflected back to me my own light. I was amazed. I found it intensely uncomfortable to have to stand in this. I wanted to turn them round until they faced the other way.

This showed me that the essence did two things: it stops us leaking our power and light away, and in doing so, by plugging the holes in our aura (and self-esteem) by that which reflects back to us our own light, it causes us to stand in the full power of who we are. We have to face this discomfort and accept it. We have to get used to the fact that we are something beautiful and precious, and stop trying to deny it.

I began to work with the two essences together, again giving them to friends and fellow practitioners for their insights and experiences. By the next year I felt strongly moved to take a stock bottle of the essence and offer it to the colony of flowers in thanksgiving; to express my gratitude for the blessings the earth had bestowed on me. On arrival I was pained and dismayed to find the colony had very few flowers this year. A fear grew in me. These were single flowers, on a single stem and this constituted the whole of that individual plant. In plucking these flowers, had I stopped the propagation and halted the growth of the colony? I ran to the other site which I had not used and found them to be as abundant as the year before. I was no botanist and could not know if my suspicions were correct at that time but energetically it felt wrong to me. I felt as if I had transgressed. Sadly I blessed the site and asked for guidance, coming home upset and troubled. Going to my therapy room I determined to sit with the bottle of mother tincture to commune with the essence and attune to my inner guidance. The bottle was on the floor, surrounded by several other bottles of the same size, in a quiet place at the back of the room. I picked up the tincture and found only the tiniest amount left in the bottom. It had a hairline crack down one side and the liquid had leaked away. Every other bottle around it was intact.

This day changed how I went on to make essences. I felt I did not want to risk the health and vigour of the plants I worked with by removing their means for propagating and their beauty. I also realised I would prefer to harness their living energy, gently released into the bowl of water. Curiously enough it was this change of direction which then led me to be able to work with more and more rare flowers, so that over time I began to understand the qualities of plants I would not otherwise have harnessed – plants which illuminate those areas of our consciousness that are less known, less common, less easily accessible and perhaps more precious as a result. I began to research ways of working that other essence producers around the globe were using – methodologies for making environmental essences and animal essences that did not require the physical properties of the essence subject in the bowl, but which garnered them from a specific external context. I also felt my way towards the bowls, wine glasses, globes I could use that would help me gently place the smallest to the largest flower heads in water, without having to pick them.

With each subsequent essence I made, I learnt more and refined the process. A sense of simple and modest ceremony began to come through and what feels like a very beautiful procedure emerged. This enables me, in the simplest terms, to tune in, ask for the healing of the flowers to be imparted to the essence bowl, and to give thanks and bring completion. With the very smallest flowers, growing close to the ground, like the precious Scots Primrose, I found ways of placing a bowl closely over the lower growing plants in order to catch the dewy 'exhalation' of the flower, which then dripped into a glass plate below. With the taller flowers in the colony, a globe-shaped glass suspended above them can hold the flower-head comfortably in water without damaging the plant. The combining of these two methods creates a full-rounded mother tincture for the essence. And thus gentle, exquisite, living essences are created. As with my earlier forays into essence making, I continue the practice of usually going at dawn (except where the essences are lunar or astrological), wearing natural clothing, avoiding touching the flower with my hand, keeping unnatural intervention to a minimum in terms of any apparatus (stones are used to balance bowls on, birch wood tripods to hold a glass), and not letting my shadow pass upon the bowl.

With the more abundant flowers (Hawthorn Blossom in particular) I was once sorely tempted to go back to cutting the flowers for these particular essences but something within me stopped me. There is a gentleness and vitality that comes from working with the living energy of the essence-subject that takes its imprint in a more numinous and exquisite way and enables us to be touched by it as living dew that nourishes our soul. Having found this way, it made no sense for me to turn from it.

And still, with each essence, the methodology continues to develop and become more refined. After all, we cannot work with essences without finding that our energy lifts to lighter and lighter levels over time; thus we keep moving towards that which gives us evermore gossamer wings to take this journey of life.

What Happens When We Take Essences?

The following sections look at the process of using essences from start to finish, supplementing the information already found at the start of the book (the **Quick Reference to Taking and Selecting Essences**), and furnishing you with a broader and deeper basis from which to work with them. Here you will find practical insights and guidance which will hopefully serve to answer the main questions that come up for you when learning the practicalities of using essences, and which will show you that you can refine things much more than the basic model suggests. There is a freedom about essences that enables us directly to tailor our use of them for our own and others' needs; to bring in our intuitive sense of what is needed this time; to listen to the response of the self to this gentle healing modality and work perceptively with this.

When we take in an essence, we are imbibing the bottled energetic imprint of the flower, gem, environment or astrological alignment from which it is made. We are not just taking some drops from a little bottle – though it is easy to forget this sometimes! Taking an essence is literally a meeting of life-force to life-force, spiritual blueprint to spiritual blueprint.

When we take an essence we are working at the subtlest and most profound levels to touch and affect levels of self which play a deep part in our conscious and unconscious behaviour. We are inviting in the innate harmony of the plant, gem, etc., to those areas within us that currently feel most dissonant. The essence's resonant accord reminds us of how the notes sound within ourselves when they are in tune and as such they help us to regain our footing. We begin to receive a gentle call internally to come back to centre; we find that we can remember the way again; the sense of 'difficulty' begins to ease.

It is important to remember this call – essences invite rather than impose. They help us heed our inner wisdom and harmony rather than bringing some external instruction to us. As the name of the LightBringer Essences suggest, they *bring* their *light* to bear so that the path back to Self is illuminated and made easier to read and follow. The actual experience of this and the resulting process is different for everyone. For many it is an internal feeling of support and empowerment: we feel lighter and clearer within; we regain perspective and find ourselves cultivating pertinent insights about our situation; we settle back inside ourselves in the place where everything fits together once more; and we are free of the mental and emotional tangles that have been confusing us. It is a lovely, light, intimate and gentle experience.

However, the essences touch each of us in slightly different ways because they enter us with a call to dance and respond, and it is up to our individual energy body to take up this invitation as it sees fit – perhaps even in ways that are beyond our comprehension at the time.

Sometimes it can take time to hear the invitation of the essence because it can be like the quietest of whispers and at first we hardly hear it and think *nothing* is happening. The LightBringer Essences have been made so lightly and so respectfully, the flowers are so gentle and, if taken as directed, then the process is a very 'soft' one which does not force anything but instead gently allows healing to emerge. Indeed we may not be conscious of any change until we have finished the bottle of essence(s) and are without it for a few days, and then we start to become subtly aware of how that thread of harmony has been holding and supporting us, its delicate quality nurturing the light in us.

It is also the case that we can initially feel discomfort upon taking an essence – in such circumstances the process does not feel eased so much as intensified. At such times the essence or essences bring forth that which blocks our healing progress, bringing it into the light of our consciousness so that we can face it and work through it. It is as if on taking the essences we have quickly found that our internal tutor – our *in-tuition* – has been turned up to full volume and we hear it shouting at us urgently. This can feel either confusing and overwhelming or like an incredibly liberating flash of illumination.

Understanding essence response, knowing how best to select them for our own and other people's needs in a way which is mindful and congruent, and knowing how to adjust things as we go along so that we can go at a pace that feels right for the person taking them, is all knowledge which is integral to working with essences skilfully.

SELECTING ESSENCES

What are we doing when we use essences? What are we looking to treat in ourselves or another? It is a common experience for people to read through the descriptions of the essences and think, 'I need them all!' On the level of thought, it is hard to see the wood for the trees; we are aware of so many aspects of our lives that can benefit from the balm and insight of the essences. But which do we really need *now*? Finding the 'right' essence or essences often comes to us in a way different from how many people assume or expect. It comes through our connection with the issue / person / energetic *feel* of the situation much more than through our *knowledge* of the essences. And it comes through our *connection with the essence subjects* (the flowers, gems, environments) as a whole and our love and reverence for them, rather than our cognition of them as little bottles of 'remedies' which are for this or that.

The following process is the one I use and recommend when selecting essences for another person:

1.   Set clear boundaries for the session – a space free from distractions which feels safe and comfortable; a set amount of time to be together (30 minutes to an hour is usually sufficient); have a pen and pad handy.

2.   Set your own private intent. I suggest the following: *Thank you for giving me this opportunity to be here with this person. I ask to be guided at all times and to support him/her in whatever way is appropriate so that they may receive the healing they need at this time. I trust that that which shows itself today is that which is ready to be met and I accept and welcome this in gentleness. I let go of my need to fix and I ask to be guided impeccably at all times.*

3.   If you have spiritual guides or mentors, connect with these mentally at this time.

4.   For the next 30-40 minutes be with the person who has come to you, listening for the nub of the issue they are facing. You may need to ask questions which will take you closer to this. Do it gently and sensitively, without pushing into places which do not feel ready at this time. It is amazing what can be achieved by listening without interrupting!

5.   At the end ask the person if they have told you everything they need to tell you and if it feels complete.

6.   You may wish to ask them for a word or phrase that sums up what they feel they need.

7.   Go to the essences / cards / book – whatever you have that represents them or is them – and ask to be shown those essences that will help the person at this time. Select these in whatever way feels comfortable to you: dowsing with a pendulum; closing your eyes and reaching out with your hands; scanning the descriptions and seeing

which essence(s) leaps out at you; seeing what page the book falls open on; taking note of any essences that came to mind as they were speaking. But as you do any of these, you are doing it mindfully. Repeat the person's key word or phrase to anchor yourself if your thoughts wander, and stay connected with how it feels to have been sitting with them in their beauty and pain.

8.	From the essence or essences that come, you have your prescription which you can now make up and give to the person, with any relevant instructions for how to take it that you may have intuited.

This process becomes easier and more natural the more you try it, and it can also be lengthened or considerably shortened as time and circumstances require. The wonder of this intuitive process is that the essences that come up can provide a reading which gives an insight into the energetic patterns and lessons the person is facing at this time. This can be incredibly comforting and illuminating. It is also possible to select essences by your knowledge of the essences themselves. As they become familiar to you, being with a person or conversing with them will spontaneously bring the essences to mind. On re-reading them you will often see why. Similarly, you can use the repertory at the back of this book to pinpoint the area or theme that is coming up for a person – grief, shock, boundaries, whatever it might be – and then reading the descriptions of the individual essences listed there, select the one or few that are most resonant and appropriate.

LISTENING TO THE FLOWER WITHIN

Whether you wish to select essences for another person or for yourself, the quality of listening needs to be the same – to listen to the flower of the inner self, in all its beauty and purity – and to listen for how best you may assist this in blossoming at this time.

Working with essences we are seeking to hone our ability to recognise our own or another person's body-being - *in this moment, as it presents*. We must become readers of energy. We sense the self that wishes to emerge, noting the obstacles that block this; the negative thought-patterns, old ways of being, resistance, refusal, fears. We ease ourselves into the sea of energy that describes to us through all our senses the expression of the Self that is seeking to manifest. We scry the soul; take a sounding of the depths; discern which way knots a person up, which way re-establishes ease and flow.

Everything takes place in hidden ways. It is that which lies beneath the surface, of which we catch glimpses through the pattern a person throws out on the surface - the circumstances that they are dealing with, the emotional state, the physical symptoms, the internal struggle, the spiritual questions – that holds the key. Connecting with this by listening to, sitting with, talking with, attending, and accepting a person, leads us to profound realisations about what it feels like to be where they are. From this we are more able to go forward intuitively and find the essence(s) because we have connected with their pain and their beauty.

When I work with someone, I imagine I am sitting in the Eye of the Paradox. On the one hand there is their pain, shadow, darkness and struggle. There is all the detritus of their life coming up and overwhelming them. On the other hand there is the beauty of their essential and undiminished nature; their unique gifts as a human being; the worth of this journey they are on; and the lessons they are currently struggling to receive. Holding both 'realities' in one's consciousness we witness both their extraordinary beauty as a human being and also their present pain. This also offers a larger space than the person may have been allowing their self to inhabit and gives them the freedom to step back into the greater clarity and reassuring calm of their eternal Self. Working from this space, what we begin to discern are the currents of energy. It is like seeing a river and - liberated from judgement, the need to intrude or to fix - it is possible naturally to observe those currents that support the Self and feel rich, generous and beautiful, and those that lead a person into stagnant pools which hamper the free flow of heart and spirit.

It is the same when we are working with ourselves. People often say that it is harder to treat oneself. Yes and no. It is indeed a beautiful thing to have someone who can see true, looking at you from the outside and understanding your pain from the unique perspective this brings. Imagine that you are a house: you know yourself intimately from the inside because you inhabit this space, and no one else can ever have that knowledge. But you have never seen yourself from the outside! So to have someone whose judgement you trust tell you that some tiles have come off or you need a lick of paint or the dark trees outside could do with cutting down to let in more light, can be incredibly helpful and illuminating. Inviting them in – into the house of your psyche – those who see true will come with candles, roses, food, drink, love, respect; they wipe their feet; they see the loveliness of you; and they offer timely and careful observations which give you the help you need to make those little changes which restore perspective and flow.

However, working within your own deep knowledge of Self and learning to trust this is also incredibly empowering. And it is done through the same means that we would listen to another. Listen as if the Self is a beautiful flower. Sit with this with utmost respect, tenderness and acceptance. Bestow upon your

Self compassion. Meet with love. And listen to the whispers of Self. Listen to the currents. Tease out what is real and what is fearful make-believe. Invite the Self out with beautiful flowers, candles, crystals, cards, a quiet space in nature, music, scents, the heart beat of the drum, crayons and blank paper – whatever feels right to you. Come to the nub of the pain, the core hurt or worry. And from here gently reach for the essences that will support you in moving and growing through this, all the richer for the experience.

Knowing the essences as mental concepts does not necessarily make for accurate prescribing or getting the right remedy. Knowing the Self and recognising Self in another *does*; listening attentively to the flower that seeks to blossom within *does*; seeking to understand what nourishment this lacks, what conditions will sustain it, what support can realistically be given at this time, *does*.

We are complex creatures. We are also in constant flux. For this reason we can recognise every remedy in ourselves because at some point in our life we will have visited that state. But at *this* time there is a particular pattern that we are working our way through, a specific part of the weave that we are perhaps struggling with. It is to this that we need to bring our attention and our love. The wounding in us will emerge and show itself clearly if it is met with gentleness and patience. Think of a small child or a wild animal that is wounded and afraid - only gentleness will allow the issue to be revealed. And in this place of sweet meeting we will find the essences emerge through our insight and intuitive knowing.

Above all it is important that we release any need to 'fix' another or to be the healer. The healer within us emerges when we have forgotten all about it, have no ego about it, but do have responsibility and respect regarding the privileged position we are in when someone reveals their vulnerability to us in this way. As we sit with a person, listening to their inner Self, we may find we release the need to *do* anything and instead become their gentle and attentive mirror. Almost without being aware of it, our hand reaches for the card or essence that is needed.

COMBINING ESSENCES

Each essence we select is like a single note which harmonises a particular area of the Being. Sometimes we only need the one pure note to touch the deepest issue. At other times the situation is more complex and we need several voices to create a chord that will bring a broader stroke of harmony and support. Usually the maximum to use in such situations would be about six. Taking a single essence can be very defining, offering a point of stillness and focus at the centre of a person's process. However, the comfort of a blanket of essences which covers all aspects is often needed in those times when everything seems to be triggered at once. Here we are able to offer a unique combination which supports the person on many levels and which offers insight into the issues and subtleties their current life lessons are touching. Where those essences have come intuitively, we also get an energetic reading of the situation which can provide additional illumination and support.

As in all essence work, there are no rules regarding how many essences to take, only the sense of what feels right in the specific context you are working in, for that person's needs, at that specific time.

The ready-made combination essences, which are a part of the LightBringer Essence range, can be included as individual essences when you are making a personal selection of essences. These combinations have all taken several years to come to fruition, at which point they are made into a new conglomerate essence by blending the mother tinctures and essences right through to the stock level. This marrying of them creates a new synergy, a new essence in its own right. As such they can be used as an individual essence alongside other essences, even where one comes up singly that is already in the combination.

HOW MUCH AND HOW OFTEN?

The number of drops to use of any one essence is generally five. Five drops of stock make up a dosage bottle and taking five drops of *this* constitutes a single dose, which would usually be repeated two or three times in a day. When combining several essences in one dosage bottle, use five drops of each to make that combination. When taking essences directly from the stock bottle, again use five drops.

This is the basic procedure in the majority of cases. However, there is potential here as in other areas to refine the process further, adjusting it to the needs of the individual and the response of their own energy body.

For those who are very sensitive to essences it is possible to reduce the number of times a day the person takes an essence, the number of stock drops that make up the dosage bottle, and the number of drops they actually take (I have given someone a dosage bottle containing one drop of the relevant stock essence, which they take once or twice daily, placing one drop on the tongue). And you can continue to adjust this down or up in either direction – lessening or increasing the number of stock drops, the frequency with which they are taken, and the amount of drops the person actually takes.

Where a person is in acute trauma, I often recommend that they take the relevant stock drops directly every half hour until they feel centred and calm again, or that they put them in a glass of water to sip every few minutes until the same end is achieved.

When working with issues which feel very deep and entrenched, especially where there is a lot of fear surrounding them, you may need to go very lightly – 2 or 3 drops of stock placed in a dosage bottle, to be taken as 2 or 3 drops, twice daily. This is gentle and effective, seeming to give the body-being enough sensitive impetus to move forward without being overwhelmed.

STOCK OR DOSAGE?

All LightBringer Essences come as stock bottles and this is the essence in its concentrated form. From this one bottle you can produce many bottles at dosage strength. Dosage involves placing five drops of stock (or as intuited – see above) in a 30ml bottle containing 80% spring water and 20% vodka or brandy.

Everyone responds differently so it is as well to experiment with this aspect of essence-taking to find what works for you. However, a word of warning: I know people who empty a few *millilitres* of stock into a dosage bottle and give this to their clients - on closer inspection it turns out their clients 'aggravate' a lot, feeling a too-sudden intensifying of their emotional state. It is important to remember therefore how very effective the essences are without a sledge-hammer approach; and how we are not trying to push someone into healing but seeking to offer a quiet invitation and reminder of another way.

That said, in general we can make a distinction between stock and dosage to begin with. The concentrated nature of stock seems to encourage a more acute and dynamic response. I advocate using this in times where support needs to be efficient and rapidly stabilising. Light Support is often needed in this way because of the very nature of it as an essence for 'emergencies' (in all senses of the word!). Dosage is gentler, softer; and to a degree we could say it is more refined. Using dosage we can employ the lightest of touches to go in slowly, deeply and delicately to core issues, without causing further fear and trauma. It feels more suffused compared to the directness of taking stock; and it offers a very respectful means of meeting someone's pain sensitively and appropriately.

However, do experiment with this. Working with some of the ways described below also subtly alters how an essence touches us. It is part of our gathering experience and skill that we develop an instinct for what method to use when.

WAYS OF ADMINISTERING ESSENCES

It is not always appropriate to give essences internally or directly from a bottle. Sometimes it is the alcohol that is the issue – though no other natural preservative has yet been found which is not either somewhat unpleasant tasting (cider vinegar, grapeseed extract or saline solution), extremely messy (honey) or which lacks the energetic value of having the essences remain in a fluid state (medicating the small white sac-lac tablets that are commonly used in homeopathy). Sometimes it is the condition of the receiver – a baby, an animal or someone too ill to be able to take the essences internally. In these cases we can turn to the many alternative ways we can administer essences.

Essences can still be given orally but in a lighter way if it is only the strong taste and nature of the alcohol that is a problem. Placing the drops in a cup of freshly boiled water then left to stand for five minutes will provide time for the alcohol to evaporate away. All that remains is a rather pleasant hint of the taste of grape from the brandy in the water. This cupful can then be sipped slowly and would constitute one dose. Similarly a dosage bottle can be made up using only spring water with a couple of drops of stock placed in this. If this is kept in the fridge, with care being taken not to have the pipette touch the mouth when the drops are being administered, and if used within two to three weeks, this also provides a way of taking the essences which has only a subtle hint of the brandy which preserves them.

Using essences externally can be a lovely way of taking them for anyone and, for people who cannot or do not want to ingest alcohol, this provides an effective alternative. Placing 5-15 drops of stock or dosage in a bath and then soaking in this for 20 minutes is very gentle and soothing. For a baby's bath, place 2-5 drops in their tub. We can use essences directly on a flannel or sponge along with hot water and do a full body rub in a morning to invigorate the body when we wake up. Similarly, a few drops can be placed on the fingers and lightly rubbed into the temples, wrists or soles of the feet.

Anything from one to ten drops of essence can be placed in about 50mls of an aqueous based cream and stirred in so that we apply essences as well as cream; or two drops can be placed on the surface of an oil-based balm, left to be absorbed in over-night and then used as normal. They can also be added to perfumes – a lovely use of either Heart Balm or Loving Desire combinations. People often say they use the ready-made Essence Mists of these combinations as perfumes anyway; but please test a small area of skin first to make sure that you do not react to any of the oils if you prefer to use these in this way.

Finally, essences can be used as sprays. Each of the combinations is available in a ready-made spray; but equally you can make your own. Simply place 10 drops of each stock essence in a 50ml spray bottle, containing 30% vodka or brandy and 70% spring water. Mist around the space you are in and/or around your aura. This is a light and subtle way of using the essences to bring balance to your own energy and the energy of your home. It is also a delicate way of using essences in a sick-room without being intrusive, though always ask permission first.

As you can see there are many options available and it is good to be creative. I use Heart Balm drops in my Christmas cake each year to create a loving atmosphere and good cheer when we eat together; some people tell me they favour Bountiful Life drops for this. Adding a few drops of essences to paint when you are redecorating the house can make a room feel very special, not to mention making the whole procedure of decorating more mindful and enjoyable! Putting a couple of drops on the top of the radiator helps disperse them through them room. The list is endless!

ESSENCE RESPONSE AND DURATION OF USE

The effect of essences *is* cumulative and we need to bear this in mind when using them. When I was first taught about flower essences, the information that was generally given was that a person should take their essences until they got to the end of the bottle and then new essences would be selected. Whilst taking them they would have the drops every day, two or three times a day. This is a good place to start as it sets up some valid principles: we generally need to keep the essences coming in once we have selected them so that they can keep incrementally heightening our vibrational response and lifting us to a more refined level where we are able to perceive and act more clearly, and we generally want to keep moving with this process. If you are new to essences or unsure about how to take them, this then provides you with a useful way to begin. However, the following examples of responses which are outside the norm, can teach us a lot about the sensitivity we can aim for in prescribing as we listen to the needs of the person taking them and their own particular way of taking up the invitation.

LACK OF ESSENCE RESPONSE
Perhaps one of the most disconcerting things when beginning with an essence is to not feel anything, especially if we have read so much about the wonderful effects of them and we have felt strongly drawn to particular ones! It can feel demoralising; we can wonder if there is something uniquely wrong with us or, even worse, if we are simply beyond healing.

In the years I have been working with essences and taking them, I have experienced this apparent lack of response myself on a few occasions. When this first happened, I put this down to the fact that they were the 'wrong essences' and re-selected. This may genuinely have been the case – I was not perhaps drawn to the particular Essence range and was just experimenting with my heart not in it. I was therefore not open to the true healing of the essence and did not accord it proper respect. I was already saying "No" to its gentle invitation at some level.

But there have been other times since when, looking back, I could see that the essences were right. So why did I not feel anything?

In 2004 when I was making the Heart Balm Combination, I began to take it myself so that I could see if I had the balance of essences right; but also because I knew I urgently needed this combination. Some of my closest personal relationships were profoundly 'out of joint' at this time; and I knew I needed to heal my own relationship with these others from within *me* before I could hope to see any improvement externally. However, as I took the essence I could feel no trace of it. This is most unusual for me with my own essences. My intuitive sense, however, was that I was to continue; I felt and heard this within myself most persistently. But to continue with an essence that seemed to be doing *nothing* when I so urgently needed *something*? I was thinking more along the lines of going back to the drawing board! I knew though that even as I thought this the process at the drawing board had been cohesive and thorough already – there was nothing left to do there. I had to walk forward and trust. After all, I had nothing to lose if this particular combination didn't work. It had not been released to anyone else and no one had been inconvenienced by it.

It was a matter of some six weeks before I began to feel the touches of this essence. I became aware of contact with my heart, not as an organ in my physical body, but as a centre of light in my energy body; not as something that was in pain and felt dark and constricted, but as something luminous, clean, rosy, divine. I found myself utterly drawn to roses. I wanted them around me everywhere in every form – as bouquets of flowers, as plants growing in the garden, as rose quartz to hold in my hand, as rose essential oil to use externally and in the bath. I wanted soft pinks in the colours around me – both to wear and in my home. As the weeks went on, I was now conscious of the essence within me and I felt comforted by its presence. After three months, I woke up one morning to find there was no issue anymore. The pain and confusion I had lived with for much of my life, held tight and defensive in my heart, had gently dissolved over these weeks. I felt the same me, but without the baggage. It was as if the lines of communication between my heart and my Self, and between me and the outside world, were now clear. I could feel a rippling outwards of this gentle rose energy and I was more conscious of being able and willing to receive it. Life began to feel much more *nourishing*.

This experience taught me how deeply we can go with essences. The most stuck and intractable situations can be eased and transmuted through the gentle and persistent use of resonant healing energies placed drop by drop, day by day, into our energetic core. For deep issues, working with a particular essence or selection in the background, and almost forgetting about it, letting it get on and do its work, is a most gentle and wonderful way to bring about profound changes in our life. In this case then, for me, changing the essences every time the bottle was finished might not have been appropriate. Instead, persistently working with one combination for many weeks was. And it was my intuition that guided me to do this.

STRONG ESSENCE RESPONSE

A strong essence response is usually dynamic and positive when it occurs; we feel the essences touch us within minutes or hours and feel ourselves moving forward and through our emotional state with their support.

Where the response is overwhelming, however, it is sometimes the case that we have not been conscious of the depth of feeling going on within us, or the profundity of a spiritual process we are in. At such times I have seen the essence take a person to the quick of their feelings, to the very heart of what is happening. This poignancy can be disturbing, especially if we equate how well we are doing with how little we are feeling, or if we are simply afraid of and unfamiliar with expressing the emotions that we know *are* stirring within us. It is important to remember that vulnerability is not a sign of weakness but of strength in a person. The *weakness* comes when we are trying to cover up feelings of wounding and vulnerability. Our strength is to be found in that moment when we admit how tough things are and how hard the process we are in may feel. From here we have touched the core of our pain and are able to start the journey back out again. Essences, it seems to me, will always help to take us back to our truth so that we can go on with our healing journey from a more real footing.

Adjusting the essences accordingly to one or two drops a day or every other day, or even once a week, will help bring the process back to one that we can manage and cope with. In all my years of working with these essences and with others, I have only once or twice observed any aggravation and have quickly been able to temper this by slowing down the essence effect through a lower and less frequent dosage. It is the beauty of essences that we have so much choice about the way we dance with them.

CONCLUSION

There are many ways in which essences can be used and can touch us. They are gentle and they are a gracious gift that invites but does not impose. With essences we are in safe hands for we are meeting on the level of energy where nothing is set in stone and where we are constantly co-creating. As we do so, we find these delicate gifts nurture that something in us that helps us to grow, blossom and bloom. The whole process of making essences is deeply intuitive. It is part of their gift then that we are brought to listen to this part of ourselves as we attune to, select and administer them. With essences we are developing a relationship with our inner-knowing which will be precious to us in all areas of our life.

Part Two
Support on Your Journey

Supporting Your Individual Path and Calling

What is and how can we recognise our Individual Path and Calling? What is the deeper Self we seek to connect with and how do we recognise its authenticity? For so many people this feels such a difficult thing to pinpoint. Let us break it down a little and look at a common spiritual technique which serves as a valuable model in helping us find this.

Our 'individual path' – the path through life that is unique to you or to me – is the path most naturally flowing for us when we allow it to be made manifest; the path of abundant creativity where it can often feel as if things simply fall into place; the way of our delight and of our freedom; the following and fulfilment of our unique gifts. Our 'calling' is the calling of our heart, that which speaks our love, our heart's desire, our passion to share and to bring forth, our love for and vision of that which is greater than our own needs. Together these two characteristics (Flow and Love) show us the way to the realisation of our uniqueness, the part we have come to play in this life that no one else can play - that singular thread of the weave, the Self.

Living from our deeper Self involves the moment-by-moment fulfilment of our loving expression and interaction with the All. Love is God, Spirit. Love is the path of least resistance (though not necessarily least challenge) and greatest joy. It is the experience of oneself as indivisible from the Whole. It is that which is individual and temporal in us, directing and directed by the Eternal and Divine. It is what we are.

Why then, if we are so intimately *this*, do we generally feel so far from the direct experience of it in everyday life and how do we bridge this gap?

We bridge this gap by stepping from our head to our heart. The process of doing this is something which, when we use techniques of meditation, we are able to see particularly clearly for here we are able to view the antics of the mind and yet quickly learn to drop beneath this and hold fast with our heart. And it is a process which is helped by the subtle and pervasive drops of living essences taken within as tuning forks which heighten our insight. With essences we can recognise the ways that lead to and from our heart and which are truly authentic to the Self.

In meditation, as with essences, we can come to know our inner landscape of mind, emotions, body and spirit, with greater wisdom and self-knowledge. When we meditate and follow our breath or a mantra, we settle ourselves into a peaceful space within; brought to centre by something that focuses our intent.

However, it has to be said that it is not always quite that simple! Many of us find, almost immediately, on sitting in quiet contemplation that the contrary happens. Our space is accosted by that which may seem to be the negative detritus of being human – the busy mind that plans and dreams; the emotions that pull us with yearnings, anger and anguish; the body that tenses in fire, shaking, pain, or just an overwhelming desire to sleep. It can be very difficult for people who are new to meditation or who are trying to establish a practice without the support of a teacher, to meet this apparent inner chaos. It feels so very much 'me' that we do not realise that it is just a dust-storm that clouds our vision and stings our body; the spin-off of a mind that needs to rest and settle, which needs the mending of silent reflection. This dust cloud and our preoccupation with it is what prevents us from seeing true. Within its grasp we can find ourselves facing deeply forgotten memories surfacing with startling clarity and vigour so that we seem to re-live events as vividly as they happened at the time. We are confronted by pain, physical or emotional, that can be overwhelming. We feel on every level that this is us and that we are this chaos. Yet it is as we persevere in following the gentle rhythm of the breath that encompasses all this and yet continues through it - coming and going, in and out - that we find our thoughts are coming and going too; an endless stream of mental patter, ephemeral and unreal. We begin to glimpse quietness within this; a pervasive peace that outlives each and every one of these storms.

The reality is that when we sit down to face ourselves in meditation, piece by piece, everything comes up. *I* have given the all that is *me*, this space and this attention, and I will be shown all aspects of myself, bit by bit. As we commit to sitting *with*, from stillness, what comes has the potential to be seen and healed, gently, day-by-day, as part of a life-long process of meeting and knowing the Self.

When I have found meditation most difficult, it has indeed been excruciating. I gave up many times in the early days as a result. It seemed pointless and detrimental to sit tense and rigid in the storm of self, with no feeling of peace. And I had no teacher to tell me how to soften to this and find the anchor within which would enable me to be compassionately present. Yet in spite of this, I still found myself regularly called back to meditation over the years until I began to sense one day that a change had occurred in me. I was aware of my heart beneath the maelstrom, and stillness beneath feelings by which I had previously been overwhelmed.

It is this stillness, self-awareness and calm beneath the drama, that we are also led to by the innate harmony and tranquility of essences. When we take them we are led back to our Self as if by a guide. Essences help us to find the shape of ourselves, to learn to connect with and heed our inner voice and wisdom, to find where we grow and blossom best, where we are flowing. Like meditation, I visualise them energetically as creating light pathways through our being that illuminate the way the Self walks. They show us which ways lead to the Heart.

DETRITUS OR GOLD DUST?

It could be said that the inner detritus that we experience in meditation is actually the gold dust of our spiritual process. The illusory part of being human - feeling we are individual and separate, fighting for the superiority of our personality, fighting to live – is set against a deep and certain knowing in our very being that we are more than this, that we are Divine before we are Human, that we are part of the loving All and not just a small, insignificant and un-cherished bundle of cells trying to survive.

The dichotomy of these two realities – the realm of Dualism and the realm of Unity – constantly throws up flotsam. Our thoughts wage war as we try to balance what is seemingly irreconcilable. We know ourselves as separate and yet we glimpse that we are whole.

Sometimes it is enough to drive us mad, trying to live some balance between these! But this balance, this tension, *is what Life is*. It is what we are here to dance with and find our way into and through. As we do this we learn self-knowledge, we discover compassion, we find our way to the heart of the matter again and again, and we begin to discern what is real *enough* within the illusion. We observe how the wind of life blows the illusions in and blows the illusions out again. We recognise the look and feel of dust and begin to discern the piercing clarity behind it. We find that nothing is new under the sun, the same old illusions come and go; it is the cycle of things. We begin to discern that there is a still-point within the wheel from where we can watch the dream but remain real.

In practical terms, sitting with the feel of the current drama or dream-state that is temporarily inhabiting and shaking our body, we can learn, through meditative awareness, to soften to it rather than to resist it; to rest deeper within ourselves so that we can watch the stirring of the surface water without being pulled by it. This process liberates us.

As we begin to discern our reaction to the drama from the response of our deeper Self, we begin to find a level of peace and stability within which feels strong and well-rooted. As we learn to recognise the shape and feel of some of the many transitory distractions of living and learn the stimuli that provokes them, we become more quiet, more thoughtful, better able to respond, more sure of our footing because we are less lured by that which is insubstantial and fleeting. Softening to encompass and even to bear the layers of tension and pain in our being, we find in these endless levels at which we can be more tender, more open, more compassionate. We feel the gritty relief of self-honesty as we face our emotions and our thoughts and acknowledge them with kindness and openness. We learn the response of gentleness. And as we progress – with each difficult or easy situation we openly meet, being with whatever comes to light *this* day, with our softest compassion and our most attentive listening - we somehow find ourselves resolving into an easier shape within. We find that we have a shape. We find 'home' within. We learn to identify it and feel for it in everyday life, discerning an inner congruity that is actually knowable, recognisable and deeply supportive to us as we watch the larger drama of life playing out before us, in life as in our meditation practice.

KEEPING ATTUNED TO THE SELF

The Self then is the larger authentic being that we are a temporal part of in an infinite context. Our touchstone for this is our 'small' self – the personality or ego. We can live our life only catching glimpses of our larger Self and our connection with the Whole, or we can actively cultivate this through spiritual practice; our connection with Nature; a simple way of living; loving actions; natural remedies; organic locally-produced food; minimal electromagnetic interference in our energy bodies; etc. All of these keep us light and clear in our being and make it easier to catch the breath of Spirit-in-Self. And as we catch this breath and allow it to breathe us we become a different kind of person. No longer are we trying to control, we are happy to be; no longer are we trying to plan and manipulate, we are willing to surrender to a greater wisdom; no longer are we floating dispirited and without purpose, we understand that there is a rich current to our lives and we know how to move with it; no longer are we fragmented and lost, we know how to sink within to touch the integrity of the Universe as it plays its melody in us.

I became aware one day, in my meditation practice, that I was actively starting my in-breath and out-breath. When I realised this I had to laugh! To think that I was so controlling that I would not even trust myself to just get on and breathe without thinking I had to *do* it! That I would not trust Life to move in and out of me! In order to remedy this I imagined waiting for and allowing the breath of Life to move through me as it deemed fit; to feel it fill me and leave me, fill me and leave me. All I had to do was watch the process and be with it. It is something I continue to go back and reach for when I find myself directing my breath in times of stress!

Walking in Self is walking a point of balance – it is where we both engage our awareness like a filter and yet allow what Is; it is where we act but from our yielding, our trust and our surrender; it is where we lovingly support but do not interfere; it is where we let go but in softness hold our heart open. In every moment our balance point is so fine that it is in danger of tipping. This is what gives the authentic life such a sense of refinement, poise and delicacy! This is what keeps us *awake*.

Jack Kornfield writes of how his spiritual teacher once made him sit on the edge of a deep well because he kept falling asleep during meditation. He did not fall asleep after this! We are all always perched on the rim of the deep well. And we find how to balance here through accepting, loving, learning and ultimately transmuting the little self that veils the greater Self. Emotions and bodily symptoms, thoughts and plans, are the slight and living transmitter of *Life* to human being, and with loving care we can learn this language. We begin to see that we are surrounded by information and feedback which teaches us where next to place our feet. The reactive self is the touchstone to the responsive Self. Our reactions teach us of our fears and distress, which in turn show where we are vulnerable and need to soften in gentleness. This enables us to accept what comes with quiet bravery, which in turn brings us face-to-face with Love. In Love we find our Self.

Living the Self-in-Balance, then, touches the dialogue we have with our body, with our vital force, with Nature, with our heart, with our sensing sensuality, with our procreativity, with our spirituality. It is the coming together of all of these in one wholistic force that is 'me' and being responsible for, responsive to and attendant of this. It is the journey of awareness and represents an eternal seeking and listening. It is felt as an inner stillness and acceptance. It manifests as sweetness and accord.

In any given moment where we face a choice and can feel the response within that gives us the greatest sense of harmony, here we find the way forward which is most true and generous – the path of flow and of heart. And in every moment there *is* this choice. Flow, satisfaction, fulfilment, grace, gratitude, relaxation, ease - all show us the way we need to go to move forward. Tension, suffering and the sense that we 'should' or 'have to' do something usually point the opposite way. Where we can sense that our core deeply relaxes and expands then we are sensing a better way forward. That is not to say that we won't have to step out of our comfort zone to come up to the mark sometimes; yet where this engenders fear and trepidation, there will always be a sense of reassurance within this and a feeling that one is becoming more than one thought possible as a result of this step. There is a feeling of enhancement, of truly becoming 'bigger' in some way, rather than of shrivelling beneath burdens we think it is our duty to bear. Learning to recognise this we learn a life skill, and we grow ever closer to Self.

ESSENCES TO SUPPORT THE BLOSSOMING SELF

The following essences help in this journey to become more congruent with and settled in the Self. Together or individually, they offer us insights and support and help this process to be gentle and joyful; a returning to an inner source of peace that soothes us and those around us.

Angel Star is the essence which above all others helps us to find, recognise and attend to our individual path and voice. It is the essence for regaining our inner guidance and finding our way in the dark by the light of this - a unique and unfailing illumination which is ours and ours alone. It is an essence which is deeply spiritual because of its ability to return us again and again to the Light when we feel that all around us is dark. It can be reached for during times of profound despair. It can support us when we are facing death. It helps us when we need to go back to the core of who we are in order to find our way through. It often involves times of make or break and acts like a catalyst to propel us forward.

The essence also supports us when we are being strongly influenced by others to the point where we no longer know what is right for us to do because the voice of another has taken precedence over ours. This can so profoundly pull us from our path that we become seriously lost and despairing within. By using Angel Star we are able to clarify and define once more, what is 'me' and what is another; and discern which way to proceed.

Balnakeil Bay and Bee Orchid assist us with the next step of the process which is to then realise this inner Self and path externally. **Balnakeil Bay** *is* the essence for Self-realization. It is an essence which deeply supports us in coming to a full understanding of who and what we are and what we have individually come here to do. Through this essence we are reminded of our entelechy, the unique role we are here to play, the exquisite and incomparable gifts we bring. We each have our own individual inner bliss or genius which we have come here to shine like a light. The alchemy of this discovery and manifestation is the alchemy of our life. Balnakeil Bay combines the placing of a gem (the aqua aura crystal which is said to activate the true Self) on the edge of the sea in a very beautiful bay, creating an essence which is grounding, fluid, supporting and embracing. It helps to know all sides of the Self and to bring our wholeness out into the world gently and wisely.

Bee Orchid goes hand-in-hand with this by supporting us in doing our life's work. This then is more specific. Balnakeil Bay helps us to understand more of the totality of who we are in all aspects of our being, including our dark and our light. Bee Orchid helps us to manifest the work we came here to do - our service to humanity - and it supports us in this from conception to completion. Where the way seems solitary and hard and we do not feel supported or understood by those around us; where we are struggling to bring together the resources (internal and external) we need to manifest this; or where we are fearful that we have got it wrong - Bee Orchid brings reassurance, strength to go forward, clarity and endurance. It is an essence of vision and perseverance which makes the ultimate loneliness of our time here feel full of beauty rather than anxiety and toil. Like the bee its flowers are named after and resemble, it is a plant which helps us in creating and pollinating miracles in our lives.

The two Hawthorn essences enable us to understand the nature of our heart's desire. They are like two sides of the same coin – the one being the tree's blossom, the other its fruit. **Hawthorn Berries** shows us what we truly want in our lives; **Hawthorn Blossom** could be said to highlight for us what we think we want and on which we may be erroneously expending all our attention. With **Hawthorn Blossom** we have the lovely delicate white flowers of the gnarly little hawthorn tree when it looks at its most beautiful in spring. At this time the tree is bedecked with an abundance of blossom so that it looks as if it is covered in snow. The year that this essence was made the trees were more abundant than I had ever seen. Hawthorn Blossom helps us to come back to our real needs when we are in a state of dissatisfaction with what we have. We may feel a yearning, pining, hankering for something other than what is before us. We may feel that we cannot be happy without that thing or person or experience in our life. We are so besotted with this that our life as it is loses its colour and we become enchanted by a dream. This is the essence to use when we feel that the grass is greener somewhere else. It helps us to come back to a more balanced way of seeing our world, recollecting that everything we need is here for us right now and all is exactly as it should be. This is one of the fundamental tenants for creating abundance in our lives – to understand, appreciate and accept that we have the very seeds of this here before us, if not the blossoms and fruits as well. It is an essence which helps us to appreciate what we have got and see the gifts that surround us on every level. From here we are able to move forward and manifest greater accord in our life because we are working *with* what Is rather than against it. We can truly count our blessings.

With **Hawthorn Berries** we take this a step further. This essence helps us to connect with our heart's desire, to manifest and realise this in our life, and to receive the fruits of our labour on completion.

La Meije environmental essence is for the times when we are at a crossroads in our life and facing real and profound life-choices. In particular it is where we are hearing the call of our deeper nature to take a path which looks a frightening challenge, in good ways, but which will nevertheless overturn much of our life as we know it. It feels more comfortable and familiar to stay as we are and play it safe, but it also feels disappointing somehow if we do this. La Meije helps us to consider where we are, to judge carefully if the time is right for us to answer the summons and take up our calling, and it brings reassurance and stability to us by helping us to take only one step at a time. Sometimes we are faced with opportunities which are awesome and splendid but are nevertheless not what we really need and the harder route is actually to acknowledge this and keep on as we are. The essence helps us see what is real and what is the glittering mirage so that we can continue moving to the summit of the mountain we need to be on. It is an essence which is incredibly supportive in meditation when we are beginning to glimpse the awesome nature of our spirituality. Here we can perceive that as part of everything we are inconsequential and on the point of disintegration, yet here we are also complete and infinite. This can be terrifying and awe-inspiring at the same time. La Meije helps us in such places of paradox and confusion.

Le Jardin des Alpes and **Alpine Aster** both support us in finding the space within for contemplation and review. They help us to retreat from the external drama of daily living and find a place of inner peace. They, too, are essences which support meditation and do this by helping to quieten and soothe the mind and recall us to our source. I am always pleased to see them when they come up during an intuitive selection of essences for they are a loving reminder to come back to peace and contemplation and to take the time to rest and renew. **Alpine Aster** is for reconnecting with our inner haven and dreaming. It returns us to our spiritual blueprint, our core patterning regarding who we are and what we came here to do, and enables us to bathe in these waters again and renew ourselves. It is gentle, light and subtle yet it is one of the most profound essences in terms of the gift it offers. With this essence we can strengthen our coherence with our spiritual connection in the sense of how this directly guides and moves through us. It helps us come back to who we are. It is like a sigh of relief! **Le Jardin des Alpes** reminds us to let go of external demands for a time in order to rest and regenerate. When we are overly stressed and stimulated by external factors we come to lose our quiet and our balance. We become more reactive and begin to move more and more quickly within ourselves, feeling hurried and harried by life. As this continues we come out of kilter with ourselves and forget to take time to ponder, settle and repair. Le Jardin des Alpes invites us to come back to quietness and retreat, to find the peace within, so that we are better able to cope with the external. As we do this, and our breathing slows and settles, our mind quietens, our body begins to relax, we find that the world around us slows down too and there is time to do all we need to do, and still take care of ourselves within this. I feel this essence and Alpine Aster help me to step back from making myself ill when life feels very full and busy.

Self Heal continues this theme. Self-knowledge and awareness cannot be separated from self-care! We cannot know ourselves thoroughly if we cannot tend and nurture ourselves. Self Heal is the essence for self-nurture. The soft purple of the herb's flowers, growing commonly throughout Britain and Ireland, indicate its energetic message. Purple is often associated with the higher chakras, especially the crown. The soft opening clusters of flowers show gentleness and a balance of that which is within and held private, and that which is then shown to the world. The essence helps us to balance our own needs with those of others. But at a very deep level it is teaching us of what our needs are, leading us to a deeper level of awareness regarding these than we may have previously had. For us all this is vital at this time when self-care of our energy, our soul, our heart, our spirit, our being, our bodies, is something we have largely lost our intuitive connection to and understanding of. Tending the spirit and soul is to tend our *essence*. As we learn to nurture this in ourselves, so then are we better able to nurture it in others and in this gracious planet we inhabit.

Whilst there are many other LightBringer Essences which support the Self, there is one other that is very deep acting that I would particularly like to include here. **Fly Orchid** helps us in those times when we are facing the obstructions within ourselves like dark clots of consciousness that we cannot seem to move beyond. These may manifest as intractable beliefs that are out-dated and limiting for us now; as habits and ways of being that undermine our growth; as karmic miasms that we have inherited that impact on our lives now beyond our conscious choice; as a sense of being darkly obstructed in our way forward; or as parts of ourselves that we fear and are held back by. Fly Orchid illuminates and transcends these blocks, helping us to bring them into vision, become aware of their shape and form and patterns, and to transmute them. With this essence we learn that nothing is against us, nothing is inherently negative. All is compost, all is potential gold dust. The essence enables us to approach and explore that which we have been frightened of or in thrall to, with curiosity and love. In this way we begin to reclaim parts of ourselves that have been shut off from us; we begin to know them as 'me' again and to inhabit the Self more fully. The energy of these darker areas then becomes released to life again, as creativity, increased energy levels, inspiration, relaxation, relief.

Touching the Self with essences is to bring back to our awareness the elegance of our individuality and the journey we are on. It is to bring relaxation and flow, love and gentleness, the releasing of knots and tangles, the dissolution of confusion and stress. Essence to essence we draw to our vital force the resonant harmony of the flowers and gems, and feel this harmony within. The more we become familiar with our inner harmony, the harder it is to lose it. We begin to reach for it more and more, and to trust its deep presence. The essences are always there to remind us whenever we are struggling with this, and to teach us how best to take this forward in the way which most lightly and brightly serves ourselves and others.

Essences and the Loving Heart

Essences, above all else, enable us to approach the heart in ways which are poignant and healing. As we come to meet this most intimate area of our own or another person's being, it is fitting that we do so with something that offers such respect and gentleness.

Problems of the heart manifest as relationship difficulties, sadness and grief, yearning, feelings of loss and being lost, inability to connect with / follow / manifest our heart's desire. As fulcrum for our humanity, the heart is our touchstone. When we cannot feel this or feeling it is unbearable, we must work with infinite care to heal our relationship with our heart and thus with our own humanness.

SELF LOVE

Having lunch with a friend recently, I noticed he was putting himself down a lot – something I always find so brutal. When we put ourselves down, that within us that seeks to grow, thrive and do good, is cruelly cut down and held back. Implied in this habit is a dismissal of one's Self; a lack of regard for who you are and who you are yet to become. I feel myself almost flinch when I am in the presence of this in another because it feels so damaging for that within which seeks to grow.

Speaking to him of this he responded that he had never considered it in this light before. We were exchanging therapies that day – he was working with me shamanically and I was working with him through the use of essences. We were both giving our best in care for each other's journeys. In this we were showing how precious we believe another person's healing journey to be.

Reflecting on this I said to him that I thought that loving one's *self* was probably the single most courageous thing a person can do. People are generally so willing and even eager to show their care for another but find it so much more difficult to apply this level of care to self; to love one's self as we would our neighbour. In that moment we both suddenly saw the truth of this and just looked at each other in delight! It was a moment that marked a significant stepping-stone for both of us on our journeys.

It is almost taboo – in British society at least and I suspect elsewhere – to love one's self. And it is not surprising therefore that there are many hearts that are heavy and sorrowful in parts of the world where there is nevertheless affluence, security and comfort in other areas of one's life. This undercurrent of grief and anxiety, this lack of belief and at times tortuous fear of inadequacy in one's self, is to be found in the most beautiful, successful, kind, generous and wonderful people. To love 'me' is deemed fundamentally selfish. To love me is to put myself first and others last. To love me is to *care less* about other people and thus to be careless or *un*caring.

But this leads us to a dangerous place. If we are prohibited from loving the self - if this is considered inappropriate and threatening to our relationship with others - then how do we learn to love another well? Because truly if we do not begin with our self, where all that we do is then mirrored outwards, how can we know how to go on and love another?

The notion that self-love is selfish is deeply misleading and damaging to the wellbeing of the psyche. Self-care, self-respect, self-awareness are *all* self-love and they are in turn the basis for self-worth, self-knowledge and self-responsibility. We need this inner foundation in order to function creatively and joyously in the world. Walking without these gifts, we walk blindly; and in our blindness we knock and stumble against others. We hurt and are hurt by our lack of surefootedness and our irreverence for our own divinity. We are limited in the love we know within ourselves and so we are limited in the love we are able to feel and respond to in the world around us. As such we are closed to it and it does not resonate and ring out through our being.

'Selfishness' is actually the expression of a lack of self-love. We only grasp love, grasp money, grasp time, grasp attention when we are malnourished from within. This is not a natural state; it occurs because we are empty - impoverished in our spirit, lacking solace and sustenance in our heart. We seek to take externally what we have not given ourselves internally.

This self-denial is causing hearts to cry out in pain. We become locked into a belief-system, behaviour, and ultimately a way of being that does not serve us. It stifles and reduces us because we are limiting our own nature out of fear of being labelled self-absorbed. Selfish and self-absorbed are symptoms of lack of self-love and self-awareness. They are not labels that are given to people who are able to love themselves. Around such people we will invariably feel loved - the natural extension and external manifestation of the love they know within.

LOVING OTHERS

Our relationships with others are definitive mirror-images for us – they impeccably reflect our relationship with our self. As such they teach us boldly of the areas within where this self-love is lacking! They show up our fears and insecurities, our blind-spots, our arrogance, our self-denial – and also the areas where we are very much in the flow and at one with life.

How then do we read this, work with this and help bring healing to this level of manifestation? The more clear and aligned our energy, the more quickly we will manifest clear mirror-images in the world around us. Our flaws will more dramatically present themselves but also be more quickly – and honourably – resolved. Our successes will flourish and thrive more easily.

'Reading' our relationships gives us information which can lead us to acknowledge their significance and richness in new ways. By understanding the apparently external as not separate from us, but a part of our own wholeness, we can begin to embrace that which we would treat as 'other'. This is where living from within the reality that *we are all One* becomes truly essential and of real pertinence in our daily lives. All of Life is interconnected, mutually dependant and all is energy at its core. We are constantly interacting with, affecting and being affected by Life on every level, in every moment. We are not separate. Yet we live as if we were and as a result we do not cherish the whole in ourselves and ourselves in the whole. We do not comprehend the awesomely intricate beauty of existence that pertains to us, is us and continues from us. In every decision and movement we are charging the universe with our energetic choices; contributing, defining, asserting. This is a gift of exquisite delicacy, subtlety and power. To learn to use this – to learn to play our part in the whole responsibly – we must come from our heart. We must read and respond, from our heart.

In our relationships this is truly played out – the tension between the individuals and the whole; the people involved and the relationship itself; the separation and the oneness. And it is this tension that allows us to grow, that marks the way and secures the boundaries so that we do not dissolve. What is most hidden in us becomes glaringly obvious in another. And what we do not give to ourselves another will very clearly not give to us either.

At a recent workshop I was attending I was seated next to a man who, under his breath, kept muttering and answering the questions other course participants put to the speaker. He was extremely distracting, not to say inaccurate and annoying! At one point he turned his attention to me, nudging me to ask again a question I had put earlier. I was clear it wasn't the right time to repeat it and didn't feel the need to interrupt, knowing the speaker was going to address it at an appropriate point later on. I tried to communicate this to my neighbour but he persisted in nudging me every few minutes, writing it on a piece of paper and thrusting it in front of me. I then tried ignoring him but this only made him worse - in this he proved the point beautifully that 'what we resist persists'! Eventually I found myself moving out of irritation and into self-reflection. What was this annoying persistent man telling me that I needed to be aware of?! Immediately the answer came to mind: I had been critical and fretful myself of late, and needed to settle back and find my connection with my inner peace again. My intention in coming on this course had been to give myself time to reconnect with this. My neighbour was obviously helping me stay with this focus!

A few minutes later the speaker naturally came to my question and answered it. The gentleman beside me fell silent. Howeer, whilst he undoubtedly had his own habits and patterns of behaviour going on, I had come to realise by the end of the day that he also fundamentally wanted to ensure that everyone was attended to, answered and cared for - he was the person who washed everyone's pots after dinner and who stayed at the end to tidy things away.

There are two main ways in which we can understand the mystery of our relationships. In any given situation which feels tense and difficult we can look at how we are not giving love to ourselves and / or how we are not giving love to another. In *A Course in Miracles* there is a wonderful phrase: 'The only thing lacking from any relationship is that which I myself have not brought to it.' This concept is incredibly empowering. The *only* thing lacking from this relationship is that which *I* have not brought to it. So where a relationship feels unsupportive, unloving, unkind, where is my support, my love and my kindness both for the other and for myself? Am I being uncaring and neglectful with them? Am I ignoring and casting aside my own needs? Within *this* moment in *this* relationship, I have the opportunity, capacity and wherewithal to bring the quality that is lacking into this situation – to relax what is tense, soothe what is fraught, step back from what is escalating, bring warmth to what is cold, bring softness to what is harsh, bring realness to what is delusional, bring boundaries to that which has none, restore integrity to what feels morally unstable.

Each relationship shows us what we hold back and what we give. They offer us the potential to fill in those areas that we do not 'own' – that we project outwards, unconsciously regarding them as either the responsibility of another or someone else's flaw. By owning the wholeness of our interactions, we move beyond a vision of 'self and other' or 'us and them', to one which sees us as aspects of each other constantly interconnecting, dancing and learning. Where we soulfully and with awareness tend to our self and our needs, we are more likely to meet this from those around us, and we are also more able to attend to theirs because our own needs are met. When we are 'full' we have something to spare, to give. When we are empty, depleted and without reserves, we need to hoard what we have. We become desperately self-centred because we are in a place of lack. When we take time to regularly and creatively refill and refuel our selves at the levels of heart, spirit, soul and body, then we remain replete and well-nourished.

THE SUPPORT OF ESSENCES

Taking essences we allow the scintillating and heightened energy of the flowers to raise our own energetic vibration and help us connect more fully with the subtle and numinous beauty of the heart. Their luminosity supports ours. Through them we begin to gain familiarity with a more grace-filled place within ourselves. Drawing on their delicate and divine energy we start to reach for this more easily, deeply and steadfastly within ourselves. Our heart becomes home; our awareness finds its seat here.

Many of the following essences are found in the combination, **Heart Balm**.

HEART ESSENCES

Alpine Willowherb is appropriate wherever there is pain and hurt in the heart. This is for the heart that is bruised to the heart that is broken. The cross we each bear is touched and transmuted by this essence. Taking it, our intention is to heal these hurts, to soothe the heart and to move on. Its gentleness and softness enable us to approach these areas which are often rigidly guarded and bring new warmth, light, insight and comfort to them.

Partnered with **Bluebell**, the two are an incredible combination for situations where we have been hurt by loved ones, to the extent that we find it hard to love again and to trust in the love of others for us. Bluebell is indicated where we feel let down, neglected, abandoned, betrayed or bereft. It is where love has apparently proved unreliable in terms of that which we have received externally from others – parents and siblings, friends, partners, spiritual leaders. This may not have been their fault but their going or the lack of security in what they have been able to offer has nevertheless caused a shockwave in us where we deeply question whether we can actually trust and rely on the love of others. Alpine Willowherb and Bluebell together help us to restore so loving a connection with our own heart that we inevitably find we are able to create strong, stable connections with the hearts of others. We begin to trust in love again because we find it is within us; from here we find it is all around us; from here we find it is in everyone we meet. As we engage with our heart in this way, it becomes a natural progression to engage with the hearts of others with such trust as well – knowing and accepting that we are all beautifully flawed, imperfectly perfect.

People seem to love Alpine Willowherb and Bluebell and often feel an immediate accord with them. With Alpine Willowherb, to find something so poignant and non-threatening, so balm-like for the heart's pain, feels very precious. A lady told me that she felt she could bear the touch of this essence in her heart at a time when she could not have let anything else in. It is gentle, kind and will not harm. Bluebell then helps us turn back towards contact with others and to share our beauty and trust. Who does not love a bluebell wood, its gentle perfume and loveliness?

Primrose essence helps us to establish and maintain relationships which are loving, healthy, mutually respectful and nurturing. It helps us express love appropriately, and receive appropriate expressions of love from others. What does this mean? It means that we do not invade, intrude upon, neglect, betray, undermine, scorn, abuse, etc another person – nor do we resonate with or attract that in the actions of another. Instead, it is as if the essence helps us to re-tune our radio frequencies to those which are, at the very least, respectful and at most, tender, warm, affectionate, loving, joyful and sensitive. The essence helps with that space between the two people in a relationship – the space of relating. It enables us to gain insights into how we act, think and feel towards others, our unconscious behaviour patterns; and how another person in turn relates to us. And it helps us to see from a clearer space within whether this is appropriate for us and for the relationship. It is an essence that supports the healthy expression of love and helps us to move away from unconsciously unhealthy patterns which may be destroying something very beautiful. By staying with the love we feel for another in our core, we can begin to see how best we can show this love in a way which actually supports and upholds us both.

Greater Cuckooflower is also an essence that supports this day-to-day relating and one which in turn helps us to ensure that we are tending our relationships and keeping their magic alive. Greater Cuckooflower assists us in being open to the intimacy of friendship and family relationships – the give-and-take sharing of the heart, the daily cultivation of trust and respect - expressions of love and kindness that enable these partnerships to grow and deepen rather than stagnate. The soft open flowers of this plant cluster together with lovely golden stamen at the centre of each delicate blossom; its rich pink colour striking against verdant leaves. It beckons us to soften, open, trust and reach out. It is a lovely essence for wherever there are family troubles, or if someone is finding it difficult to make or keep friends. Partnered with Primrose, it helps a person establish very loving, supportive relationships with good boundaries and a kind of robust and beautiful tenderness at centre.

At a deeper level, there are essences which enable us to tend to our heart spiritually and energetically. **English Bearsfoot** essence helps to cleanse the heart of deeply ingrained taints of negativity. Where a person is very heavy-hearted (Alpine Willowherb, Bluebell) and this has led to a dark, somewhat bitter outlook on life, English Bearsfoot in combination with these other essences will cleanse, lighten and rejuvenate the heart energy. This plant flowers in the depths of winter, with a host of fresh bright lime-green flower heads which are in stark contrast to the dark ground below. It cleanses, aligns and restores the equilibrium of the heart's energy and expression. The miasm of loss, disappointment, resentment and despair that can cloud the heart, is gently cleansed and released by this essence so that the heart's fresh beauty can be felt and lived once again.

With **Scots Primrose** essence, the diminutive jewel-like richness of this flower enables us to embark on a deeper journey of the heart – to uncover the true treasures that lie within us as we learn to love more deeply, with greater compassion, forgiveness and empathy. It teaches us of unconditional love and a love which is strong enough to endure with hope and gentleness. It helps us become truly soft enough and vulnerable enough to deepen and grow in times of pain; to become more infused with Spirit. In combination with some of the more acute heart essences (Ruby-in-the-Storm, Alpine Willowherb, etc.) to help heal that initial loss, Scots Primrose then takes us further to within the deepest recesses of our hearts where we find the ability to draw strength and beauty from the situation we are in – and to come through.

Alpine Forget-Me-Not and Grand Quintile both teach us of Divine Love. **Grand Quintile** helps us reach beyond the boundaries of self to the energetic reality that underpins everything – that we are all One. To live this reality and move beyond the illusion of separation and division requires a profound change in our innermost core, a shift to seeing life as a Divine Harmony of which we are a crucial part. This essence helps the concept become reality so that we are able to live within this, rather than simply view it as a mental construct with which we have sympathy. The gentleness of this essence brings an expansive, embracing and supportive energy – it can feel like a web of light upon which the heart chakra can become more solid, more glorious, more light. In a similar way, **Alpine Forget-Me-Not** teaches us of the love that permeates all aspects of our existence, so that we begin to know this as an everyday reality. It is an essence which helps us to realise that Divine Love just is, and that we are held by this all our lives. With this surety, faith and love can begin to replace fear, for what is there to fear when we are divinely guided and protected? Through Alpine Forget-Me-Not we find that all the love we have ever given or received is always there for us to draw on. No matter the external circumstances, Love itself, at the core of any and every relationship, does not die. It is simply there to be uncovered, so that it may breathe new life in to that which has become stale on a superficial level.

These latter essences are profound ones – not to be taken lightly. Their work is often deep and takes time to reveal itself. They reach into us to touch and reveal our most beautiful heart-felt expression of humanity as we each hold it. They are not flowers or crystals which impose or force – they simply invite us to evolve by suffusing us with their gentle harmony and the signature of their loving presence. In this they gently tune us to their benevolent vibration and light.

With all the heart essences, it is a journey within; a commitment to exploring, clearing, knowing the truth of and bringing tenderness to the heart of who we are. Wherever you are on this 'path of heart' the essences will gently assist you and hold you in safety, enabling you to keep placing one foot in front of the other, connecting you with the internal illumination that eternally lights the way.

Your Sensual and Sexual Essence

It is a gift to find that in the world of essences we can touch this most intimate area of our lives with gentleness and efficacy. There are those who are lucky enough to not be confused by the myriad strange messages that these modern times bring us regarding sexuality; but for many of us this is not the case. We only have to walk through a city, look at a magazine stand or turn on the television to be infiltrated by a hundred messages daily, some subliminal, some not so. We see them in media, read them in fiction, observe them in clothing and advertising, hear them in conversations, wonder at them in jokes. For many of us, men and women alike, expressing our sensuality and sexuality joyously, healthily, safely, vivaciously in these modern times, in ways which fulfil ourself and our beloved, is a challenge, and even – at times - an unknown. There seems to be no solid, rich archetype within our society to draw on – male or female - unless we are fortunate enough to have this within our family or community.

This is the area of our lives where incredible tenderness, union and bliss can be reached with another, but also where the most horrible and terrible crimes are committed against another human being. All of this is held in our collective psyche. And at some level this impacts on us, stirs us, brings up questions, and ultimately calls on us to seek answers. Our challenge is to reach for answers which can enrich and truly serve us in this time, rather than deplete us, degrade us and take us into despair.

Our sensuality is a gift of beauty. It is the coming together of our individual senses in a rich dance, and it is a fertile luxuriating in the ways in which we touch and are touched by this physical world. It is that which returns us to ground, connecting us deeply to our body - a most reliable anchor; and that which enables us to rise on the contours of our feelings - alive to the colours, textures, tastes, smells and sounds of life, and imbued with them. And as our senses come together in dance and accord, full of the life we are living, we are led impeccably to that numinous other sense which transmutes us and defines us - our inner knowing.

Our sensual nature is the doorway in - the means by which we connect with who and what we are. It is that which teaches us we are truly alive and that which enables us to engage with this on every level and understand the richness. Our sexuality is the deeper place of our carnation, creation and ongoing dance with the fresh rebuilding of our ancestry. It is where we take the seed of our self forward and trace this through our future, either as physical, emotional or spiritual progeny: adding to what we have been given; changing and transmuting it by our love and our expression; co-mingling with the love, future and creativity of our beloved; daring to place ourselves at the apex, suspended in time, so that we may once again dive into life, warmer, brighter and sacred. We engage with and become engaged to the life-force.

So how does knowing this help us practically to move beyond fears, insecurities, guilt, negative patterns, boredom, longing, aversion or a demanding desire? What is the path back to reconnecting with the sacred sensuality in ourselves and in our relationship with our beloved, to a rich and fulfilling coming together of body-with-body if this has gone amiss in our relationship? And how can essences assist us?

Sex arouses strong emotions – not all of which are positive. Overwhelming fear can be experienced by men and women alike when their experiences or images of sexuality have been negative or abusive. Incredible insecurities abound about 'performing' as we see the gods and goddesses of the movies offering us distorted or too glossy images of how we should look, how this should be done and how perfect our bodies should be, making us feel impotent and insufficient. We can feel guilt and shame at sullying our bodies with these earthly desires which we secretly believe may be impure and which some religions morally ring-fence and control. We may feel confusion because we wish to co-create a loving connection with the one special person in our life yet constantly see the ease with which relationships are abandoned on screen and in fiction – an ease which has filtered through to our societies - so that we begin to feel if it is not working, that we should just 'move on'. Yet this does not satiate the hunger in our soul for deep connection. We feel disturbingly out of control of and out of touch with our own bodies because of all the above and hardly even know what it wants or needs. Our modern-day diets can lead to our body feeling dry, infertile, impotent, over-caked with saturated fats and with foods which have no life in them, so that sex becomes painful, bothersome or not even on the radar. Or we feel completely at the whim of desires which burn us with their heat, are purely physical and leave no room for connecting with ours and another's heart, being and soul.

This is not just an individual problem. It is something which touches us all and which touches our young. It touches our connection with our life-force and the healthful guarding and procreation of this for our futures – on all levels, mental, emotional, spiritual and physical. And it touches our ability to feel afire with the creative potential of being alive, resourceful, seeded, begetting, renewing – a human who is fully present, vital and *being*.

RECOVERING THE SENSUAL

The path back begins with reconnecting with our own sensuality first and foremost - to understand the dips, peaks, troughs and wellspring of this - and thus go on to reconnect with the sensuality of our beloved. As we foster these closest relationships – that of our self and our love - our understanding of humanity as a whole, and of the universe of which we are part, becomes richer and deeper. We can *start here* and it is an internal process which nothing needs stand in the way of because we are free to go at our own pace and uncover our own sweet step-by-step liberation.

Recovering our own sensual nature is to restore our awareness of the interaction between our body and senses, and the world. A few evenings before writing this, I was out late taking my dog for her last-minute walk before bed. It had been a grey wet Cumbrian day such as we had not seen for a long time. Everything was saturated, dripping with moisture, branches limp and drooping. As we walked along the lane I had my big coat on, hood up, huddling out of the rain. Then something began to pierce my defences. I realised it was actually only drizzling now, a few stars were even out, and the valley was still, immensely quiet and peaceful. I had come out expecting rain, guarded against it and almost missed what was. Putting back my hood I breathed in the moist clean air and the loamy, smoke smells of the fires burning in the houses, felt the peaceful sanctuary of darkness, turned my face to the light rain and looked up for the glimpses of stars in the sky. I took in the looming comforting shapes of the buildings nearby and felt something in me relax and expand. I smiled broadly at the secret beauty and stillness of the evening, feeling touched and restored by the world.

Five, six, seven years ago, I was in such a busy stressed place in my life that I couldn't make this sort of connection at all. I couldn't feel Nature's touch, I couldn't slow down enough internally to let it in, I couldn't get beyond some kind of internal wall of busyness – and I felt deeply bereft and helpless. As a child I had always loved these sights, sounds, smells – that incandescent feeling of standing in the garden at dusk and it *changing*. How could I have lost this?

Coming back to our sensual self occurs in the smallest but most meaningful ways. What we are looking for is that which is right under our noses. We are not on a search for the Holy Grail – though we have a very good chance of finding it on this path – we are on a search to re-inhabit and reclaim our living presence in the physical world. We are remembering and restoring our right to be physical and to be moved by what is; to dance and delight in; to reach towards; to be inspired by; to contribute to; to revel and play in. It is our reconnection with the joy and innocence that exists in all of us when we stop and actually look at the amazing world we live in. Its beauty is both unexpected and reliable; deeply restorative and nurturing. Being touched by the rain reminds us to open our senses to these caresses, to this liveliness, to this communion. Seeing the beauty in a loved one's smile, as if for the first time; creeping downstairs in the dead of night for a drink or a snack and being struck by the peace and stillness of the house; savouring the smell of a lovely dinner cooking, bread baking, a cake rising in the oven; receiving an affectionate card; buying a present thoughtfully and joyfully; nurturing a plant back to health; feeling the thrill of riding the waves of the sea, climbing a mountain, riding a bike; enjoying using beautiful tools or instruments which are hand-crafted for their purpose and which sing to our touch. All of these are ways in which we experience and enjoy the sensual in ourselves. What is their key? We are touching life-force to life-force. We are stepping outside that more recent human world where we are deadened and numbed by artificial lights, air, music, production lines, deadlines, etc. We are choosing instead to meet on the cusp of creation, savouring what exists and seeing the imprint of what is possible, taking time to let ourselves bleed into the fabric of that which surrounds us, and finding our way back to ourselves subtly and profoundly changed. We give ourselves the gift of our own living physicality, allow it to go out, touch and experience, and come back saturated with light and life, teaching us of the gifts of this world and our place in it.

The clothes we wear with their fabrics, textures, colours, matching of colours, feel, function, appeal, flattery of form, feeling of rightness – this is just one area in which we have endless choice to express ourselves and nourish and delight our soul. Here we *dress* our soul. We give it the apparel that chimes with us today. We go forth with a sense of rightness and wholeness because we have given ourselves the gift of self-recognition. Choosing clothes that are hand-made, or well-made, that don't involve the slashed prices and slashed lives of sweat-shops, that use natural breathing fabrics, that have soul, that take us away from wearing always black, grey or navy blue, that add a dash of panache, that imprint a smile or elegance or comfort or safety or daring upon us for that day as befits our mood, that subtly transform us and take us into more of who we are, that hang on us like a mantle of gentleness, power and completeness, that uplift – these are all ways in which we can apply our sensuality in just one area of our life. And there are so many other areas: eating the foods that nurture, please the senses, stimulate the appetite, bring us back to our core self, restore our energy, relax our being; taking care of our home which can reflect in the most simple or complex ways all the subtleties of our desires to create a safe and nurturing space in which to be; carving out beautiful moments within our working day - adding plants to our work area, adding kind words to our interactions, including a dose of buoyancy, enjoying good listening, delighting in small treats of food, meditation, a walk in a beautiful place, speaking with consideration and from an inner wise knowing, laughing regularly and inclusively.

We have so many ways to touch, be touched by, create and luxuriate in. We can change the very air around us with the slightest gesture if it comes from our living heart. We can meet it from the rich grounding of a sensual being, open to this vital communion.

As we regain this sensual connection, this sublime and subtle empowerment, we inevitably begin to ignite a fire within ourselves. There is a quickening, an excitement, a stirring. And others recognise and are drawn to this too.

We begin to inch towards our own self as someone who is capable of handling the sensual and sexual, for we are reconnecting with the ways in which we can take a sounding of ourselves, in which we want to be and know others can be; where we can meet in a spirit of adventure and trust because we are not dependant on one other to satisfy our soul, are not bound to another's destiny, are not required to depress and suppress ourselves to accommodate someone else. We know we are meeting delight to delight; in respect; with listening, seeking and adventuring; moving in, sensitively moving away; heeding the call and answer; two people on a journey where they are happy to collide and conjoin but as it suits the innermost sanctity of one's individual path and being. We can love most generously when we are not jettisoning our own soul in the process. We take a sounding, re-assess, trust, speak true, act true, begin again.

In recovering the sensual self we recover our passion for life, our *joie de vivre*. We come to re-cognise the life-force and light in all that surrounds us. We see where this is clouded over by layers of maimed, damaged, wounded living, but nevertheless still exists. We begin to develop a trust in the quality of vivacity that permeates us all and to know that this can be fully returned to us. And we come to a place where it is easier, more natural and more kindred to reach towards another.

LOVING ANOTHER BODY AND HEART

Without our internal sense of wellbeing intact, it is beyond difficulty to meet another, never mind conjoin with them through body and heart. Thus that reconnection with this in oneself is so fundamentally important. But as we move towards this, we can begin to repair, create, dance with, explore and enjoy our relationship with our beloved, especially through our sensual and sexual meeting.

How do we create a loving physical relationship that sustains and fulfils, and is richly and fluently intimate, for the long-term? We begin with the now. Here as I meet you now, my beloved, how best can I respond in trust and love, with affection and joy? How can I enjoy you, enjoy us, feel the gladness in my heart for what I first saw in us and what we have built or have the potential to build together? In each moment, asking oneself how to love with body and heart the other, how to receive that which feels most beautiful and nourishing now, how to continue to plant and grow green shoots within our relationship – all this brings back a fertility to our lives together and a stability that is not staid but that allows an increasing level of natural change, depth, and togetherness as we move through life.

To touch gently with love, the everyday caresses - gently stroking a sore back; moving hair out of the eyes; placing a lovely mouthful of food in another's mouth for them to try; kissing on waking, on going to work, on coming back, before going to sleep; strolling along hand-in-hand or arms round each other; hugging; rubbing the feet; playing with long hair; swinging each other round – all of these are ways in which we weave our contact with each other's bodies. The more mindfully and lovingly we do this, the more we enjoy it for it takes on a richness and intent. It feels good. These are pure expressions of tenderness for each other - a physicality of the everyday sort that nevertheless leads to deep intimacy. Our touch for, with and from our beloved is not the same as the caress we would give another, for we do this with our beloved knowing we always dance on our sexual and sensual connection, the well of intimacy that exists between us. When ignored, this troubles and disturbs us; these are as dark waters that shift uneasily beneath us and we have no means with which to navigate them. We dip in, we fear we are drowning, we will barely take our toe there, or we are consumed by it. But we have not perhaps found a way to let these waters add their moisture, their life-giving drink, to our daily living together. Our sexuality is kept separate and apart; alien; fearful.

Weaving a daily love - safe contact, soft touch, sensual connection – creates a web that holds us safe and beloved. What stifles sexuality is, on the surface, being too tired, too busy, too unwell, too infrequent, too demanding, too violent, too critical, too uncaring. With all of these, the absolute vulnerability and trust that a sexual relationship requires becomes too frightening a prospect and we create our own defensive ways of dealing with this. Sex is not a means to intimacy in itself. Intimacy is created in the everyday, in the soul, in the loving touches and words that support and uphold each other, in the thousand daily ways we can reach out and say, without words, 'You are special to me, I want you in my life, I enjoy you being here, I love you, I want you to know this, I want to explore life with you, I want to be with you.' We love actively and engagingly and draw ourselves and our beloved together. And we are naturally drawn to go deeper, to connect more, to have one thing lead to another, because this is a body we know and love as well as our own, and with which we live tenderly on a daily basis. And as we do so we find we are recovering the art of communicating with each other, sensually and sexually, lovingly, lightly, and within our joyful capacity at this time.

The following essences will help to illuminate this further and bring insight and flow to this process, guiding us to recover and reconnect with the authentic, joyful essence of our own sensual nature.

ESSENCES TO SUPPORT OUR BLOSSOMING SENSUALITY AND SEXUALITY

The majority of the essences given below are found in the combination, Loving Desire (see **Combinations** for further details on how to use this and understand it is a conglomerate essence in its own right).

Pink Purslane and Aragonite are two essences which help us to return to our bodies and reconnect with our sensual needs in ways which feel safe and enjoyable. This is an authentic return to 'how my body expresses itself to me, how I listen to and heed this, and how I may walk forward in this in a way which enables me to relate lovingly and expressively with another'. **Pink Purslane** is a lovely delicate plant, relatively commonplace, growing on river banks and on damp ground. It is low growing, with light hairless foliage, and star-like flowers of the softest pink. It is an essence for the everyday touch of intimacy and love in long-term relationships. Something bright and beautiful, but commonplace – not to be afraid of, avoided, destroyed by harsh treatment, or trampled underfoot – simply to be tended and enjoyed. It helps us to return sexuality to that which is part and parcel of our daily lives; a delicate, robust and joyful flower.

This is a useful essence wherever there is fear of sexuality and physical intimacy; where there are long gaps without sexual contact between couples; where a wall has grown up that shuts off the life-force of this gentle flowering. It reminds us that we are safe to love and be intimate; that physical touch can be wondrous and breathtakingly beautiful; that we can meet our gentle beloved in this space if we trust. Where there has been trauma and abuse in the past, this will help a person to move away from those destructive patterns of sexual expression and dance a new and more loving dance. Used as a single essence in a spray or taking internally long-term, Pink Purslane helps bring both liberty and stability to a long-term loving commitment with another as the couple finds they now have permission to love each other in full tenderness. Even just one person taking this in the relationship will enable deep changes.

Aragonite helps us to be embodied. This is not about our sexuality and sensuality as such – though it is the precursor to this – it is about feeling safe enough to inhabit our physicality fully. For people who are in their head, or more comfortable in spirit than in matter, this essence gently guides one back to the soft warmth of the body, of home. Aragonite can be used wherever there is profound disconnection from or fear of one's physical body. It helps us safely and gently to know the gift of being a physical being. It provides a way back in when we have been severed from this. For people who have had near-death or out-of-body experiences, Light Support and Aragonite can be used in the acute and long-term to restore a safe connection with being back here.

It is with **Dark Red Helleborine** that we find the mystical and sacred centre of our sensuality and sexuality. This is an essence which draws us back to the hidden, mysterious, yet-to-be-revealed nature of this aspect of ourselves. This is a journey which never ends, a power which is never fully known, but which necessarily becomes more and more intimate and essential to our daily living the more we embrace it. Not simply as sexual expression – though this is a rich and vital part of it – but as the kundalini force which connects us with our deepest power and sensitivity as a human being. By connecting with this we connect the dots, we bring together in union the energy of all our chakras through the central axis at the core of our body - the spine - and in doing so we realise and become imbued with the rich power of our life-force.

The beautiful flowers of Dark Red Helleborine are richly coloured in deep claret-red with gold at the centre. They appear hidden and secretive, growing up and around the tall slender stem, each one an individual clot of colour. The plant grows in limestone grikes and is rare. It seems almost subdued in appearance at first; but when one looks closer it is seen to be incredibly beautiful and elegant.

This is an essence that allows us to approach our sexuality with the rich merging of the physical and the spiritual. It leads us to the body as the gateway to a spiritual store-house of undiscovered energy; our physical and experiential contact with Source. And it helps us if we are discovering this through practices of tantra, kundalini yoga, etc., or if we are simply and gently journeying for ourselves back to our sacred knowledge of our bodies and our life-force. Experientially we begin to feel the fire that is burning in us, the life that is coursing through us, and we begin to reconnect once more with how to wield and dance with this. One lady who took this felt like she quickly regained contact with a powerful, almost feline aspect of herself, and began to move in and be aware of her body in a much more sensual way which was enormously enriching. And a young man who had been working with tantric yoga practices for several months reported that when he took this essence he realised that he had focused too much on the goals of energetic power and physical prowess which can come from this discipline. With the help of Dark Red Helleborine he found himself turning to a softer practice, one which nurtured a more feminine, embracing aspect of himself and which led him to what he called, 'a more delicate and rewarding contact with Spirit'.

As with Pink Purslane, Dark Red Helleborine is the other flower essence that really helps us return to our body and its mysteries, ecstasy, play and joy. On a specifically sexual and sensual level, it helps us find our way back to exploring these joys and wonders.

For some there is guilt and shame associated with sexuality. This may come from upbringing, religion or personal experiences. Bodily desires are felt to be base and lustful, with nothing elevated or even tender about them. For some they are perceived as a means to an end, purely physical gratification. For others there is little or no enjoyment because it simply feels like something that pulls them out of and away from the more refined energies of spirit. Dark Red Helleborine and all the other essences mentioned here help with restoring a balanced connection between body, heart and spirit. However, **Chickweed Wintergreen** helps specifically with the issues of shame, guilt, of feeling unclean, of feeling tainted. This is an essence which helps energetically to wipe the slate clean, to bring absolution and the restoration of energetic purity. In relation to one's sexuality, whether shame prevents one from going near any kind of physical contact, or spoils what you enjoy because of past associations and negative experiences, this essence will help resolve this and bring healing to the psyche. The lovely pearlescent flowers shimmer amongst the woodland undergrowth in the forest. As an essence its touch is cleansing and uplifting. It lightens the burden and releases the taint of guilt.

Vernal Equinox also supports this. The gorgeous blue and green gem combined with the green energy of the Spring Equinox, offers us an essence that is both stabilizing and renewing. It is an essence which particularly pertains to the sacral chakra and its effect is to wash clean, revivify, release tension and blocks, and restore flow. It reconnects us with the juice and joy of life. Just as Aragonite helps us to feel comfortable with our physical body and return to it our energy and presence, so Vernal Equinox supports us in returning to the sacral chakra specifically. This is one of the areas of the body that has the most problems in modern times, especially for women. Menstrual, hormonal, reproductive, sexual and lower digestive tract difficulties can each indicate congestion and energetic trauma in this area. Bringing the gentle strength of this essence to support the sacral encourages this area to flow and flower once more.

With **Venus Transit** we take this further. This and Dark Red Helleborine together make a wonderful combination that feels mystical and potent. Venus Transit is an essence of beauty, richness and passion. It restores us to the luscious fertility of the Divine Feminine which is within us all, connecting us to earth and nature, to our own creativity, and to our power to birth and destroy. It is an essence to use where there is a lack of connection with one's passion, one's femininity, one's rich beautiful aliveness! The essence is one of only two LightBringer Essences which had a flower floating in the bowl. On this occasion I was strongly 'told' to do this in the internal communications which take place as I make an essence. The essence was made during the Venus Transit of 2004. Three bowls were placed on the ground: one for the energy of the feminine; one for the energy of the male; and the third, which contained the single bloom of the Burnett Rose (*Rosa pimpernellifolia*), for the sacred union of both. In each, the planet's trajectory across the sun was mirrored in the water.

This is an essence which restores our connection with the energy of the Goddess and enables us to let go of places within our being where the masculine energy has been like a strait jacket. It restores us to the sacred heart of the feminine; to its beauty, sanctity, nurture, deep empathy and exquisite sensuality. When 'She' within us is able to be in balance and in equal power, we feel a sense of relief, of proportion, of right relations restored. When I made this essence I had a profound sense that we were safe once more, that the Feminine has returned and her tenderness and power will be felt again. I felt that when I rested back in this deep pink energy, I was utterly secure and nothing need phase me, ruffle me, or seduce me into old patterns of fear because the feminine is rich, life-giving and life-affirming and she holds us all. Virgin, Mother, Crone, Goddess.

ESSENCES ON THE BODY

Using any or all (as found in the **Loving Desire Combination**) of these essences enables one to regain a healthy, playful and loving connection with one's sensual nature. There are many ways to take them. Some people find them quite strong and begin with one drop once a day, or even once a week, diluted in water if need be.

I recommend using them in the bath; using them in a cream with some delicious sensual oils and rubbing them into your sacral chakra, lower back and thighs; using the Loving Desire mist and spraying them around the bedroom regularly and particularly when you wish to connect with your partner sensually; misting them around the room you are eating in before a romantic dinner; placing the stock drops in water and sipping them daily; or using the drops in water-colour paints and creating mandalas which explore your sensuality - whichever way feels most enjoyable. For women spraying the mist on the inside of your wrists (check that there is no reaction to them by doing a small spot-check on your skin first), on your neck and even through your hair can make a light and lovely perfume. All of these are ways which are subtle and creative, and which help you explore your relationship with the essences and the insights they are bringing you, returning you to your body as you do so.

The body is our spiritual home, our sensual garden of delight, our beauty, our manifestation, and our early warning system. Connecting to this more and more, with tenderness, exploration, care, delight, and respect, we create a link between ourselves and the rest of physical reality which is gorgeous, multi-sensory and amazingly rich and alive. We also ensure our future as beings who are able to celebrate and reproduce their body wisdom for the generations to come. The following visualisation helps you to meet with the layers of your sensual/sexual self and discover that which may block the free and loving expression of this in you. It is an illuminating journey, bringing great insights and healing.

VISUALISATION: The Pools of Sexuality

Prepare a comfortable quiet space for yourself, where you will not be disturbed. You may wish to use candles, incense, soft music, etc., to create a sacred place. Have a sheet of paper and pen to hand, with your intent written at the top. Think carefully about this as this will anchor you for the visualisation process. I suggest something simple such as: 'INTENT: To understand and bring healing to my sexuality.'

Read through the following visualisation. Then simply close your eyes and follow the process described here – or get a friend to read this aloud to you whilst you journey. When you have finished, do not speak. Write down everything you remember from the visualisation.

Close your eyes, turn your attention inward and let your breathing become slow, regular and peaceful.

As you settle, you begin to see a landscape emerge before you in your mind's eye. You are standing in an alpine meadow half way up a beautiful mountain. Soft cushioned grass surrounds you, delicate wild flowers, moulded rocks which are warmed by the sun; and the sky above is blue and peaceful with occasional birds weaving a pattern above you. Around the clearing are some large fir trees, tall and blue-green. A gentle breeze blows through them causing a soft murmuring. You can hear the sounds of marmots, crickets, bees and birds.

To your left you see a small path which leads round a corner, out of sight. Remembering your intent, you follow this path and find before you a gorgeous pool. This is a place of great peace and contemplation. You feel instantly at home here.

You are drawn to the pool's tranquil surface and move closer to look within. Now the journey begins.

As you look into the pool, you notice the colour of it as it appears to you. You find yourself drawn in and, though you are standing safe beside it, you find yourself merging with the pool and being taken within it. Here you meet the first level of your sexual self. You are taken into an image which reveals this first level to you.

By your side you find that you have a guide. This person or animal or being, is someone you instantly trust – you feel you know them at a deep level.

For the next minute you explore this level and your guide shows you how to understand it. You are shown that even if an image appears frightening at first it cannot harm you – it is simply a teaching tool to bring you enlightenment. Your guide holds you steady, the pool keeps you contained and safe.

When you are ready you withdraw from the pool and find yourself once again standing by the edge in a beautiful safe space.

If you need to, you can return to the meadow you first came to, to rest and restore yourself. You will find guidance there on your return if you need it.

When you are ready you continue.

You look again into the pool and this time the colour has changed and you know you have reached the second level of your sexual self. You find yourself drawn in, though you are standing safe at the side of the pool. You begin to merge with the water and see an image appear before you which reveals to you this second level of your sexuality. Beside you your guide stands, loving and gentle, to help you with this wonderful journey.

As before you spend a minute exploring the image(s) you see before you and then gently return again to the pool side, in the beautiful mountain range, where you are held and protected as you seek your deeper knowing.

Continue in this way until you have explored all three levels of your sexuality. At any time you can return to the meadow to speak with your guide, receive healing support, take time-out and restore yourself in the peace of that alpine clearing.

When you have finished, return to the meadow for a final time. Ask your guide to tell you if everything is complete and to help you if it is not. Thank your guide.

Return to this reality and write down all you remember from this journey – the colours of the pools, the visions, the guidance and your feelings. Anything you do not understand immediately will come clear to you in time. You can return here whenever you wish to consult with your guide, restore yourself in the alpine meadow, or revisit any of the pools of sexuality.

The Energetic Self in Trauma

Essences help us to connect with our own essence and, through the joyous expression of the flowers and gems and environments they come from – these jewels of Nature – to shine with the light of this. Working with them over the years has taught me again and again of the beauty that lies at the centre of all situations and of all hearts when we are open to seeing this and reaching for it. Sometimes it feels impossible to do this, for a situation simply feels too hard and too brutal in our lives. But even the most tragic and painful situations ultimately yield their gifts, as do some of the most difficult relationships.

So many times I have heard from clients in deep pain, and endlessly experienced for myself, that as we come to the nub of the situation and explore it fully, the lesson at the core is miraculously a gentle one – often we need to do some simple things like relax, yield to our inner knowing, move forward lovingly in the way which sets us straight and authentic within our being. We can let go of that which has been making us feel pushed, harried, crooked, less than or past ourselves, and come back to our truth. Resistance causes us to suffer as we fear and distrust our inner voice and try to move against it; as we do what we think we should but confuse the burden of duty with the liberation of fulfilling our responsibilities. Releasing our resistance and listening in to our inner nature and judgement shows us something deeper and lighter, and helps to set us true again.

To find our footing is to find the way which releases us from burden and pain. Our burdens and our pain actually come, not from responsibilities or difficult tasks, but from our fear and resistance to what Life brings to us and our reluctance and lack of confidence in participating with this. I have had the experience of fulfilling the most mundane tasks and finding them a solace during busy times because their familiarity and the sense of routine are both soothing and productive, and they give me time-out to let my mind wonder, daydream and repair the damage caused by too much hustle and bustle. This is only a small example but significant. And larger happenings in our life are often made up of these smaller choices that precede them.

Any and every situation invites an inner listening, within which is the potential for re-discovering or taking forward our feeling of accord with Life. How do I balance in this moment? How do I meet this next opportunity to dance on the paradox of living and feel my poise and my authentic stability? In Haven Trevino's book *The Tao of Healing*, based on the Tao Te Ching, he writes in verse 73,

> *All that has happened,*
> *Has had to happen.*
> *All that must happen*
> *Will happen.*

It is a profoundly simply and reassuring truth! No blame, no guilt, no recrimination, no resistance – just the simple fact of Is-ness, of Being, of Living. In this moment, we are exactly where we must be. It is something we can either dance with or flounder in. But it Is, regardless.

When we are faced with trauma we are also faced with our vulnerability. We find our sense of our life and reality jolted out of recognition, sometimes irreparably, and we experience the distress and confusion this can bring. Trauma, shock, profound change – even when essentially positive and even when consciously chosen – can be deeply challenging. In such circumstances the sense is that we are being thrown into a realm beyond our ken, where the known becomes unknown, and that which we have familiarly recognised as self and the humdrum of our everyday life, becomes subtly and disturbingly distorted.

The more fleeting shifts and changes of everyday life are naturally met through our innate ability to endure, learn from and ride the waves; our ability to cope with the majority of what life brings us. However, the deeper pain of profound trauma and change, the likes of which truly takes us past ourselves, brings us to another level. It is here that we can particularly reach for and utilise the gentle touch of essences to help us find out way through.

When facing severe trauma, extreme pain and intense loss, we need an equally extreme response – *profound gentleness*.

In Jack Kornfield's beautiful book, *A Path With Heart*, he writes,

> *Every spiritual life entails a succession of difficulties because every ordinary*
> *life also involves a succession of difficulties, what the Buddha describes as*
> *the inevitable sufferings of existence. In a spiritually informed life, however,*
> *these inevitable difficulties can be the source of our awakening, of deepening*

wisdom, patience, balance, and compassion. Without this perspective, we
simply bear our sufferings like an ox or a foot soldier under a heavy load.

To see challenges as healing opportunities, as gifts of Spirit, as fertile ground for enrichment and greater maturity, is to turn around our sense of things being done to us and, as the writer Byron Katie puts it, seeing it as something that is done *for* us. Through trauma and change, where our world is rocked and we are washed up on the shore of our most intimate vulnerability, we have profound opportunity to gain strength, wisdom and deepening love. It is here that we can become both more real and more realised as a human being, here that we have the opportunity to surrender deeper in our core, as fears and shadows within come to the fore to be borne and blessed.

This takes enormous courage. When we are faced with the loss of a loved one, the destruction of some beautiful and beloved part of our life, the destabilising of our essential security, how and why would we see any of this as good? The spiritual perspective that Jack Kornfield refers to holds within it a resonant sense of 'rightness' - but in reality can we reach for that?

When we are in pain our instinctual defensive response is to guard against what is happening, to tense, to become foetal and curl in on ourselves, to lash out at that which seeks to open us up. This is the child in us that dominates at this time, the part within that feels most powerless and most buffeted by the world. We do not think we can do anything to affect what is happening so we go back to previous patterns of reaction when there was someone else to take care of things for us. We blame – ourselves, our loved ones, the person who 'did' it, the world, life – because we cannot bear the apparent senseless pain of it otherwise. But in this we see ourselves as separate, viewing life out *there* as something other than life in *here*. We feel the victim. We forget our own power, creativity with and collusion in Life; the moment-by-moment interaction and dance that we are in and of; the wholeness that we are hologram to. We are incapacitated and blinded by our sense that the cruelty of life has dealt us another blow.

Yet, returning to the spiritual reality that Jack Kornfield, and every spiritual tradition, speaks of - the real question is perhaps - how can we *not* see the good in what comes to us? How can we, after going down the blind alleys of tragic and painful responses so many times before in life, not come to see that this creates its own tragedy? How can we not see the utter weariness of this road that offers so little light or joy? We have reacted with fear, distress and rage enough times in our life to know how powerless and spent this leaves us. We have defended ourselves in every conceivable manner and yet feel no safer. We have shut off anything within us that might be vulnerable yet feel no stronger. We remain alone and deeply fearful of the next assault; in the dark, unable to integrate and assimilate what comes; unable to differentiate, unable to discern.

Choosing another way, we consciously act to stay *with* what Is rather than shut off from it in fear. When we are faced with a situation that is painful, the living and vital potential in us to stay present and open is always there: to soften to life; to return to the heart. We can become aware of the fearful tightening that takes place within us and meet it with gentleness and understanding; to bring our attention to bear on what is; and to continue lovingly to yield, explore, be open to Life. As one spiritual teacher famously put it, 'In our defencelessness our safety lies.' This 'other way' is more real and profound, but also lighter and more life-affirming.

When we view changes that come as another aspect of Life unfolding to meet us, we alter our perspective but we also open up our ability to respond. We find there is room to breathe in a situation which may previously have felt tight and claustrophobic, hemmed in by fear and dark thoughts. By staying receptive to what comes, by bringing continuing awareness, by returning ourselves again and again to Love and the Divine, we reclaim time, space, insight and choice. We reclaim inspiration. We reclaim the seat of our heart. To paraphrase the poet, Gerard Manley Hopkins, 'I greet the Divine as I meet it and bless where I understand'. In this greeting and gratitude we are given the key to go beyond the pathos of our individual human suffering to see something larger, deeper and broader. Here we go beyond limitations and defences that need to be guarded and upheld twenty four hours a day, to a way of being *with* Life that enables us to be receptive to its wonder and miracles; which genuinely and grittily offers us hope.

Many times, I have observed how those who stay open, true and vulnerable in the most harrowing times come out deeply strengthened in their wisdom and integrity, in their beauty as human beings. There is a depth to them that instinctively draws us; a humility about life and a sensitivity to the cares of others which makes them precious indeed to know and name a friend. The person who can forgive the murderer or the country or the government, or whoever is perceived to have held the weapon and the power that has warred with and killed their loved one, the person who can embrace them and keep their heart open to them and make steps to know and love their enemy, is the person who knows and feels within them true justice for they have kept themselves open to the experience and offered their vulnerability and their confusion. They have chosen to tread and know more intimately the path of their heart and they have elected to work with the justice of a higher authority, knowing they do not need to judge.

On the other hand, where there is a fear of engaging with the pain, and the person shuts their heart down in bitterness and/or despair, it is anger that seems to carve them rather than gentleness and they can become desperately stuck in their wounding. This is a most painful and dark place to be.

A wise friend often used to say to me when faced with something challenging and painful, 'You have a choice. You either harden or you get softer. It's up to you.' In other words, we can either let ourselves be burst open by this and deepen to our vulnerability, or we can shut down, shut off, guard against. In Stephen Mitchell's translation of *The Tao Te Ching* he writes in verse 78,

> *The soft overcomes the hard;*
> *the gentle overcomes the rigid.*

The Tao Te Ching is full of such wisdom – a wisdom that speaks of the direct experience of yielding to the mystery of life, standing quietly by, watching from within, being with, listening and learning of the pattern of things, knowing when to move and when to wait. This softening is not weakness but the true courage to stand and face what is and stay light enough in the heart to be able to bear it. We have this potential in every moment and every situation, and the choice to be this way. It takes practice, patience and awareness.

I recently went through a trauma that shook me deeply with the sudden loss of a dear friend. Within a very short time I could feel an insidious sense of desolation and helplessness beginning to take hold of me. I felt the strong and magnetic urge to capitulate into being a victim of the situation, especially as it came at a time when things already felt difficult and challenging. This was, potentially, yet another blow.

However, the loss of this beloved soul was the loss of someone I love dearly, who I knew had loved me dearly in return, and who had been an integral part of my daily life for a long time. In the shock of grief it was nevertheless this love that shone and endured. Over and over I took my self, the flood of poignant memories of my beloved friend and my feeling, into my heart and into this love. A moment-by-moment process. I felt the grief. I felt the intense pain of the everywhere-absence of him. I felt the inexplicable shock of him being there one moment and gone the next, with the confusion and numbness of this. The place that could hold these feelings with any degree of comfort and solace was the quietness at the centre of my heart. This was also the place I felt closest to him when I was most acutely feeling the loss of his physical presence. It was to here that I kept returning. In time I began to see that I was not losing him. Here in this inner sanctuary he remained, even though my memories began to fade – far too quickly it seemed, overprinted by everyone's joint memories of him and by photos which only capture a second not a context – and here I was able to let go of trying to hold him, knowing he never could go from this place of Love.

Anger, frustration, regret, guilt all comprise the complexities of grief. Rejection, confusion, and the raging questioning, *Why*? Being with this with acceptance and understanding, as best as I can, I have felt more able to see that these emotions will pass in time and that they do not in anyway supersede the joy of having known this lovely being, nor will they long hold out against the enduring pleasure I can even now feel of remembering the many ways in which our lives touched and changed each other.

If suffering comes when we resist and judge that which happens to us, then our way to move beyond our suffering is to bless it with acceptance and compassion as another part of life which comes to us to seek our healing love. I remember hearing the Chinese spiritually instructive tale of a man whose son has an accident whilst out on his horse and is badly injured. The villagers commiserate with the old man but he simply says, 'Some say good, some say bad.' A few days later all the able young men of the village are recruited for war. The villagers exclaim at how blessed the old man is for his son is unable to go. He quietly replies, 'Some say good, some say bad.' When trauma and change comes, we cannot *know,* we cannot say if this is good or bad for we have no idea of the ultimate plan and shape of things. *We do not know what is written.* What we have is a choice: to judge from our immediate feeling reaction and determine our world from there; or to sit quietly and wait for our wisdom response.

The reality we live in is one of unity clothed in the tension of opposites. We inhabit the world of Yin and Yang at the temporary material level. At the spiritual level we are of and one with the Unity that transcends this. This tension between these levels of reality – the apparent that we touch and sense with our physicality and feel the impact of in every moment, and the deeply divine and intangibly known that whispers in our very cells – is the point upon which we are all dancing. We stand on this apex, this Paradox, whether we are conscious of it or not; and the climax and interplay of this within our being is what constantly calls us to determine our selves - *as we see fit.*

Where we can meet it, we can exchange gifts of love and deepening understanding and come away fulfilled. This is because we have opened our hands to both sides of life and embraced them – the hard and the soft, the harsh and terrible, and the lovely and delightful. It is not possible to be full if we only wish to look at that which pleases us in life, if we shun the dark and fear its touch. We come away fearful and uneasy, having set the shadows murmuring. To live avoiding death, not looking this in the face, is to live on the run. Yin and Yang *are* the unity. Destruction and rebirth *are* the wholeness of Life. Not one or the other!

ESSENCES TO SUPPORT BREAKTHROUGH

Using essences in situations of trauma and distress we instinctively draw on their light; the imprint of stability we can feel they hold; their divine and individual expression that has flowered against all odds; their fullness; their loveliness; their sensual comfort; their life-giving breath; and the fragrance of their Spirit. These are things of beauty and life that we know will help us to pull through. They are vessels of the essential and numinous quickening that comes direct from the core of what Is. They help us to feel this in ourselves.

When I speak with people who are in a very difficult space and who have lost hope, who can hardly bring themselves to take even essences, I often say to them that by the single act of reaching for them they will affirm their healing, for they have reached to touch something light in the very darkest of times. In itself this is an act of defiance and of hope. With this done, the essences can then begin to work within, helping to restore solace and balance, illuminating more clearly the path through.

The combination, **Light Support** is specifically for times of distress and trauma, for times which feel dark and troubling. It emerged from a period in my life when I was going through incredible darkness, struggling in my very core to find the light and have it radiate in my life once more. I also kept meeting people who were suffering in a similar way and who also needed a particular kind of support. As a combination it had to be able to touch the depths of desperation and sorrow and help a person come out the other side. As such it has a vivid luminous presence and a gentle and reassuring touch. It is called Light Support because it supports one's inner light and also because its energy is very gentle, whilst nevertheless feeling firmly grounding.

Light Support can be used in any acute trauma. It helps to centre us, stabilise our auric field, strengthen our connection with our true Self, and heighten our ability to find our way in the most confusing and overwhelming times. In this way we feel more able to cope with and respond to the situation we are in, rather than being thrown and buffeted by it. This is incredibly empowering. Wherever we need a 'rescue remedy' – in an accident, after bad news, when we have suffered physical injury, in acute grief, when we are in shock, etc. – we can use Light Support.

People often comment, on taking Light Support, of the sense that their Crown chakra has been cleared and opened. Also that they feel more grounded and rooted again. These are two of the main reasons the combination feels so stabilizing during times of distress. Often the Crown chakra shuts down in trauma because we go immediately into fear and this in turn cuts us off from our spiritual connection. Simultaneously we feel emotionally 'thrown' by what has happened, as if 'the rug has been pulled from beneath our feet' and quickly lose our contact with the Earth and thus our grounding. **Grass of Parnassus**, **Golden Light** and **Angel Star** in Light Support, profoundly connect us with our crown chakra and help keep this contact strong and bright, maintaining an open chakra and the ability to stay channelled in Spirit. **Ruby-in-the-Storm** and **Scots Pine Sentinel** – the gem and the tree essence respectively - help us stay deeply connected with the earth. Combined, these five essences hold us to our central axis at the core of our body which in turn keeps our chakras in communication and balance with each other, holding us directly aligned between Heaven and Earth. Rather than being thrown off-course, we are held firm energetically and so are able to respond to what is happening with greater clarity and composure.

There are many situations then in which we can draw on this combination. When we use essences in an acute situation we are using them to prevent the trauma continuing, staying held in our energy system to be carried into the future. The residues of past traumas can colour our beliefs and actions in our life now and can require our attention just as strongly as new traumas do. Many of us carry wounding in the form of emotional, spiritual and mental scars where we still hold and feel the fear of the original distress. This leads to a kind of chronic shielding of parts of ourselves that are still vulnerable and have not yet been tended and healed. Taking essences at the time of trauma prevents this happening. We can also reach back to old traumas, taking essences for longer-term situations which are still needing completion. By reaching back and touching the original pain, administering the solace that was not present and available at the time, we lovingly soothe and transcend these wounds. Here we are using essences as a timeless catalyst which enables us to move through the experience held in our cells and bring resolution.

Light Support is also calming for us when we are in the throes of very strong emotions – panic, anger, grief – and feel that we will be overwhelmed by our feelings. Using the combination in such cases, we are better able to collect ourselves and respond rather than react. It seems to help us find the quiet centre within all the turmoil we are feeling, supported particularly by the gem essence Ruby-in-the-Storm. And from here we are less likely to be lured by the tempest of our passion and more able to regard it with detachment. Where we have long-standing patterns of being overtaken by particularly strong emotions, then Light Support may be combined with the relevant individual essence(s). Where the feeling is guilt, combining it with **Chickweed Wintergreen** helps bring absolution to our energy-field, wiping the slate clean from past shame and guilt so that we can move on, connected with the innate purity of our nature once more. Chickweed Wintergreen, combined with **English Bearsfoot** and

Light Support, also helps with feelings of envy and jealousy where we become consumed by the thought that someone else is better than us and where we are tainted by the negative energy this can lead to. Where there are strong and uncontrollable outbursts of anger, Light Support will do much to help calm these, being further enhanced by the addition of **Silver Birch 'Fire'** which helps us meet our anger without being destroyed by it or becoming a destructive force ourselves. Instead we begin to understand the core frustration behind it and are able to reveal the vulnerability which is otherwise covered over by the prickles. Where there is a tendency to excessive criticism of others - often a sign of our own needs not being met and resentment building up because we have restricted our own freedom and pleasures and now feel it keenly – Light Support helps bring balance and perspective. **Viper's Bugloss** can be added to make us more aware of the power of words to hurt or heal, and to learn again the sacred discourse which will empower both self and others.

Where fear or anxiety may be said to be self-imposed, Light Support can assist us, for example in situations where we are giving a public performance or going through an important event in our life. In such circumstances it is most sustaining if we can remain connected with our inner light and strength, often the part of us that signed up to put us there in the first place! Within the combination, **Golden Light** helps us to stay positive in our thoughts about the event to come by letting us see the immediate future with hope rather than fear and dismay. And the other essences combine to help us stay connected with our light and to enable this to shine forth. Placing a few drops of the combination in a glass or bottle of water and sipping it before and during is incredibly reassuring and a very unobtrusive way to take the essences.

I used Light Support a lot when I was learning to mountain bike and discovered more about the combination in these fun but challenging circumstances. Mountain biking involves cycling off-road tracks across terrain which, in my part of the world, is very rough and very steep in places. These routes can amount to little more than a jumble of rocks and pot-holes requiring absolute focus and attention if you are to traverse them unscathed. At best it is utterly freeing and exhilarating. At worst it can involve a lot of falls, bringing a profound and frustrating lack of confidence, especially when you first start out! On these harder days, falling off the bike or even just nearly falling off, could leave me badly shaken, making it hard to keep focused. This could lead to further disasters along the trail if I did not quickly get myself centred again. I learnt to reach for Light Support at such times and found that within a minute or two I was back to centre and able to continue calmly again. With time I have grown more proficient, enjoy mountain biking very much and still nevertheless take my bottle of essences in case there is a situation where I am shocked or hurt. After all there is always the return journey to be made and it is preferable to be centred enough to get back in one piece . . . ! Since then I have learnt that there are comparative situations in every-day life where we need to avoid 'further disaster along the trail' by collecting ourselves quickly when we take a 'fall'.

A final use that is most poignant as regards Light Support is to spray it in the room of a person who is ill or, in particular, when someone is passing or has just passed over. Light Support Mist has the effect of clearing negative energy in a room and/or in a person's aura, of dispersing darkness and of nurturing one's light. It helps you to feel lighter, uplifted and cleansed. At times of death and illness a great deal of fear can be felt by both the 'patient' and the family and carers, resulting in negative discharge into the ambient energy-field which can lead to an oppressive atmosphere. It is, for many, a time of anxiety, of facing mortality and loss, and of feeling great uncertainty as what lies ahead appears so incredibly alien and unchartered. The mist can be used and the drops taken regularly to help bring spiritual and emotional sustenance at such times, to clear space for the Light, and to remind us that all is well and we need only to trust in and go with that which is unfolding. By clearing the build-up of negative energy each day from the room, the spirit of the person who is ill has space to breathe and reach for higher levels of energetic support. It helps to bring reassurance for all involved and allay fears and worries that come from our attachment to our physical body. From a spiritual perspective we are able to view this journey differently.

In any situation of trauma and distress then, I recommend that you reach first for Light Support within the LightBringer essences. This can be used every few minutes in the acute and then several times daily for days, weeks or months, as long as the situation remains, until you feel once more reconnected with your light and inner clarity.

Further solace can then be given to calm the energy body and heal deeper pain and distress once the shock has worn off. This is detailed below.

THE HEALING PROCESS

The **Healer's Light Combination** supports us in the process of actually healing – be this physical, emotional, mental or spiritual. It helps to reconstitute the energetic matrix that enfolds and encapsulates our physical being where this has been damaged or distorted. It is an essence which holds the blueprint of health and healing, where Light Support holds the blueprint of a stable and aligned auric field. With Healer's Light we are reaching back to the most subtle levels of the auric field where the pre-physical map for our entire being is held in the Universal Energy Field. The combination then helps bring this harmonious patterning through again to grosser levels of physicality.

What does this mean in practice? We can use Healer's Light wherever we are struggling to begin, maintain or move forward on our healing journey; where we are dismayed by ill-health and feel unable to cope with it; where we get so far in our recovery but then keep slipping back because we lack either the knowledge or the discipline to gain any ground. It is an essence which helps us to understand what health is and how this feels in the nerves and fibres of our being. It assists us in finding within ourselves what *cure* is for this individual in this situation and supports us in moving consistently towards this. Sometimes healing needs to occur primarily on an emotional and spiritual level, sometimes on a mental or physical level. In all cases, all of these levels are touched to a greater or lesser degree, and it is our understanding and insight around this that helps us to move forward. The feel of our vital force within us, how it moves through and shapes our entire Being, and how we respond to or resist this, is the teaching of this combination.

We can use Healer's Light at the acute and chronic levels to help us move fluidly towards new levels of energy and wellbeing; to connect with the inner resolve which will see us through to the forming of new, more healing habits; to accept more quickly the resulting higher energy levels we will attain; to help with the establishing of these in our cells and energy matrix; and to adapt naturally and positively to more healthy ways of being. Sometimes we seem to resist achieving greater health. Many people find it very hard to change long-standing patterns which will nevertheless bring them to a level of much greater comfort in their life. This combination helps us to move beyond self-sabotage and to establish a dialogue between ourselves and our body so that we are able to maintain a living and vibrant relationship with our life-force.

As such it is a tonic for healing. It is a combination which brings us firmly back to focus on this and which affords us much more insight and awareness. For maintaining the health we have (i.e. to protect ourselves against sabotaging, undermining or being energetically contaminated in our health) or for regaining it, it holds us to our life-force and its teachings.

Healer's Light includes several essences. To start with **Lady's Slipper Orchid** is a plant with an incredible presence. It feels dynamic and vital. It reminds us of the life-force within ourselves, strongly reconnecting us with our healing potency. As such it is an essence which helps to restore our belief in our ability to heal when we feel despairing of recovery or unable to see the way forward. It reminds us of the feel of our vital-force within and helps us to attune to this and move with it, strengthening our connection with our ease rather than our dis-ease.

Spring Greens is a gentle environmental essence which brings an energy of great tranquillity. It helps create the internal and external environment that is truly propitious to our healing, that which is soothing and balm-like to our nerves, and which enables us to relax into and surrender to the healing process. Within this tranquillity, though, there is also all the energy of spring – of bright renewal and regeneration – coiled and waiting to be released. It restores us to our awareness of this within ourselves.

Butterfly Orchid is an essence which clears the energetic channels within our body and our subtle energy-field. It strengthens the pathways for healing energy from Source to come through us so that we can utilise this for our own healing and/or for the healing of others. This essence helps us truly to become a conduit, able to open ourselves to Divine energy. It is an essential essence for healers because it enables us continually to channel clear, light healing energy rather than use our own more limited resources. In this way we become a more authentic vessel for healing because we are open to a higher level of guidance and energy; and we also take better care of ourselves by not giving away our own energy, becoming tired and drained in the process. For those who are in the position of being healed, Butterfly Orchid helps us to receive healing energy and not block this in our physical or auric body. We are better able to accept light into our being. The flower this is made from is very pure, angelic in its feel, delicately scented with a honey-like fragrance, and exquisite to look at. It holds a very fine energy which in turn refines our own energy-body and lifts our vibration.

Bogbean essence again assists both those who are practitioners and those who are in the process of healing. It helps to uphold the healthy gathering of information through all our sensory capabilities. Many people can feel overwhelmed by how much information they can pick up through their senses – including what they can pick up of other peoples' energies. For practitioners they can often feel they are too sensitive, absorbing like a sponge the energetic discharge of their client's pain without being able to protect themselves. Bogbean, in combination with Butterfly Orchid, particularly helps with this by establishing a kind of energetic boundary which can retain its individuality and integrity without merging with the client's. However, it is also the case that, as patients, we can feel this overload of information and not know what part of it to trust or act on. Bogbean helps us discern the information that is truly of use to our healing and wellbeing; recognise that which supports our health; guard against that which we do not need to 'take on'; and cultivate both the stability and sensitivity in our energetic antennae to be able to move forward mindfully and wisely.

Self Heal is the essence of self-nurture and, without this precious essence, this combination would be incomplete. Self-nurture is self-love is self-healing. And self-healing in turn is the beginning of healing the All that the Self is part of. The other name for Self Heal is All Heal, indicating its deeper lesson. Self Heal reminds us of the vital need to nourish and tend ourselves on every level, to listen to our healing needs, and learn the discourse of our body and being that teaches us where healing lies. We cannot heal without caring for and loving ourselves; and for those who feel this is something they are unworthy of this essence provides a vital support. Without the fundamental self-belief that we are worth the effort, we will not accord ourselves the respect and attention we need to maintain full health. Nor will we be able to assist others. Self Heal helps us to establish a tender and practical relationship with our Being in all its entirety and to learn how to treat ourselves well, coming back into harmony as we do so. It is a most invaluable essence.

Herb Paris touches us at the pre-physical level to recreate the harmony and structure that underpins our auric field, bringing this through to the more physical level of our being. It is a gorgeous cosmic green star of a flower. Yet the flower is almost disregarded when you see the plant as you pass by because the leaves beneath it are so large and coarse, initially claiming all your attention. Herb Paris is about the design behind the coarser physical level. It affects the layers of structure in the auric field which are precursor to the physical body. With the gentle insight the essence brings to us we are reminded of what it is to connect with our inherent structural harmony and balance. It helps us skilfully to re-master a sense of what health feels like in the systems and cells of our body and intuitively to work with this. It supports our energetic matrix at its most subtle and intricate levels, helping to bring strength from this higher source through to every level of our being.

The combination Healer's Light is for those who are being healed and for those who are helping others to heal. It is for when we are working with others and need to reconnect with what *health* is and for when we need to strengthen this connection in our own process. It is for aligning ourselves with the light of healing. The combination can be used to help intractable cases where hope has been lost and the nature of healing has been forgotten somewhere along the way; or during times when we simply wish to remind ourselves to walk the path of our healing lightly and joyously.

Healing is a living, vital process which encapsulates the innermost dance between Self and Life. It is the dialogue of body and soul, the constant feedback loop that teaches us the how, where and when of our response to life's challenges. It is what keeps us spontaneous, authentic and happy, and enables us to thrive in this life. It is a dance to cherish and become deeply familiar with, rather than to fear.

With essences we can move through trauma with greater inner stability and lightness, feeling the beauty and potency of the essences as they hold us safe in ourselves. We can treat what is now, what has been and what is yet to come. We can sprinkle these dew drops of Nature where they are needed to re-harmonise and rebalance. The following visualisation is one which helps us to create a simple ceremony around this process when we need to seek support from the essences. It can be adapted to any time and can be as simple and short, or as long and complex, as we like.

VISUALISATION: Divining Your Healing Light

Prepare a comfortable quiet space for yourself, where you will not be disturbed. You may wish to use candles, incense, soft music, etc., to create a sacred place. You will need a set of essences that you are familiar with, this book, a pack of essence or angel cards, some runes or some other means of divining that you trust.

Have a sheet of paper and pen to hand, with your intent written at the top. Think carefully about this as this will anchor you for the visualisation process. I suggest something simple such as: 'INTENT: To understand my healing needs at this time / around this issue . . .'

Read through the visualisation below then simply close your eyes and follow the process described here – or get a friend to read this aloud to you whilst you journey. When you have finished, do not speak initially. Write down everything you remember from the visualisation.

Close your eyes, turn your attention inward and let your breathing become slow, regular and peaceful.

As you settle, you begin to feel yourself go more deeply within. Your breathing becomes slower and the tension eases from your body. You begin to move towards your centre.

As you do so you feel the emotions that have been filling you begin to show themselves. You may feel some of the stronger, more difficult emotions you have been trying to avoid. But beneath these may be sadness, vulnerability, tenderness. You may feel bruised.

As you connect with your emotions and let yourself sink softly into their centre, you feel the shape of this issue as it is for you, the reality of it as it feels for you, the nature of it as it currently lives in you.

Holding this awareness and repeating your intent softly to yourself three times, you gently reach for your divining tools. With your eyes closed, reach for your first card or essence, asking to be shown what the issue is. Place it beside you on your left-hand side without opening your eyes. Reach for your second card, asking to be shown what your fears and resistance are. Place this on your right-hand side without opening your eyes. Reach for the third card and ask to be shown what is the healing for you. Place this directly in front of you.

Sit for a moment, feeling the energy of the divination tools you have selected. Know within yourself that your answers are already before you.

Open your eyes slowly and in your own time turn over each card or take up each essence in turn. Come to the book and read the descriptions of each of these in the order in which you selected them.

Spend some time writing up or drawing the teachings this divining has shown to you, for further contemplation.

When you have finished, close your eyes again and reconnect with your centre.

Affirm: 'I move forward with my healing in peace and love.'

Repeat this affirmation three times.

Thank Spirit for the insights you have been given and gently open your eyes when you are ready.

This visualisation can be used for an issue from the past, a fear about the future or something that is troubling you in the present. It is gentle and effective and helps to bring insight as well as healing. By calming yourself and giving your attention to your process, you open to receiving help. You also place yourself in direct contact with Spirit to receive the wisdom and teaching of the issue you are facing. In this way you will see more quickly the sweetness at its centre and view it less from the perspective of something being done to you by Life, and more as something that is being done *for* you; you will have regained your spiritual perspective. If you use essences as your divination tool you may then wish to take a combination of the ones you have selected; or just take the third essence, the one for healing, until such time as you feel the issue has resolved.

Part Three
Individual Essences and Combinations

ALPINE ASTER - *Aster alpinus*
KEYNOTE: *Inner Space*

Helps us connect with our inner haven, the place of our hidden self where we have complete privacy and space to dream, grow, renew ourselves; enables us to contact our inner dreaming / spiritual blueprint.

Plant: Alpine Aster essence was made in the French Alps. This low-growing, daisy-like flower with lilac petals and a bright golden centre, grows on short turf in the mountains. The silky petals and the downy fringe around the central gold stamen give it a quality of softness and gentleness.

HEALING QUALITIES

Alpine Aster supports us in connecting more deeply with our inner haven - that part of us which is known only to Self and Spirit. Here is the space within where we are growing and incubating along the lines of our spiritual blueprint. It is a place of incredible intimacy and privacy—the store house of our own unique energy.

The essence strengthens our connection with this place that is reserved for us to be with our Self and our God. It invites us to come here to renew and revitalise our senses, our direction, and our core. It is like going on a retreat to a beautiful pristine environment in nature, where there is no one else to be found, no distractions, only the potential for a deep communion with one's self. Alpine Aster offers space simply to be—to bathe in the waters of our own spirituality and uniqueness, reconnecting with our dreams and plans, and looking deeply at where we are going.

This inner haven is constantly fresh, present and new - a space to relax, recharge and revitalise.

Indications: *Inability to rest and relax; feeling cut off from one's core; difficulty being in own company/being alone; constantly on the go; for busy times full of stimulus/worry/excitement - but with little time to connect within; to help create time for contemplation and review; for retreat and recuperation.*

Energetic: Crown, Brow and Heart chakras; intuitive faculties.

I connect with my spiritual blueprint

ALPINE FORGET-ME-NOT - *Myosotis alpestris*
KEYNOTE: Divine Love

Knowledge that we are all loved, all of the time. Remembering past love; understanding that love does not die. Opening to receiving Divine Love as a practical and real presence in our lives; receiving this nurture and nourishment at a deep soul level. Spiritual Love.

Plant: Alpine Forget-Me-Not grows on rocky mountain ledges and has distinctive deep blue flowers with a piercing golden yellow eye at the centre.

HEALING QUALITIES

Alpine Forget-Me-Not reconnects us with Divine Love – not as a spiritual concept but as reality. It reminds us that we are all part of a loving universe. It helps us connect more profoundly with this force that is beyond the level of 'human love', beyond ego, beyond personality; which is eternal, impersonal, unconditional and endlessly compassionate and giving.

Alpine Forget-Me-Not reminds us that Love is present in every experience of life - in every relationship past, present, and yet to come - and in our own heart. It helps us feel this presence, recognise its touch, and deeply relax into its care. As we begin to grasp Divine Love as reality, as the sinew and marrow from which our life is formed, we inevitably start to let go of old thoughts of being alone and isolated in a harsh world. The essence helps us live from the internal awareness that we are each an integral part of a loving creation, and to forget not to receive this divine and endless Love.

The essence encourages us to expand beyond the confines of our present perception and to embrace all the love that we have ever known, have ever been touched by and have yet to meet. It is multi-dimensional, calling us to draw on all sources of love in the universe, to connect to them and receive their nourishment. It particularly helps us to still feel the warm presence in our hearts of loved ones who have died or whom we do not presently have contact with. Love never dies—it cannot, the very nature of it is eternal - it is vast, infinite, unconditionally bestowed and ever-present. Alpine Forget-Me-Not reminds us to open to it so that it may enrich our lives at the deepest levels.

Indications: *Feeling disconnected from divinity/spirituality; unable to grasp that we are all Love and are surrounded by and imbued with Love; belief in a vengeful god; spirituality remains a mental concept but is not yet deeply felt, understood and lived; deep feelings of being disconnected from the source of Love.*

Energetic: Heart, Throat, Brow and Crown chakras; Celestial body.

I am at one with Divine Love

ALPINE WILLOWHERB - *Epilobium fleischeri*
KEYNOTE: Heart Balm

For touching, tending, and releasing deeply held wounds in the heart; brings intimate and poignant connection with long held wounds so that healing may gently flow.

Plant: Alpine Willowherb grows amongst stones and pebbles, alongside fast-flowing alpine rivers. Its rich pink flower consists of four larger pink petals separated by an equal number of slim magenta petals, so that it almost looks as if it has a cross through the centre.

HEALING QUALITIES

Alpine Willowherb is an essence for tending to sadness, pain, and feelings of being wounded in the heart. For grief, loss, separation, betrayal, neglect, resentment, or for feeling unable to forgive—it goes gently and deeply into the heart's pain, helping us to bring attention to areas we have been unable to heal, helping us fully to tend to these hurts.

Alpine Willow-herb is a pertinent and poignant essence - it touches the heart's pain with infinite care and exquisite gentleness. But it is also very direct, going straight to the site of old wounds within our energy, inviting us to feel this pain in a new way—this time softly, with acceptance and calm. As we learn tenderness for our selves as individuals, it is not unusual to experience a blossoming of tenderness for others, in our heart. The essence encourages us to open doors long closed, letting the heart's radiant energy gently reach out to touch those around us.

Alpine Willowherb is deeply supportive in any situation where we feel grief (acute or chronic) and/or where we feel the heart is closed. It is an essence to work with consistently during such times and to reach for whenever this pain threatens to overwhelm or lock us into despair. It brings lightness, tenderness, and acceptance, and helps one uncover gifts of insight often at the centre of such wounds.

Indications: *Grief and loss, acute or chronic; feeling of being deeply wounded in the heart; sadness which does not shift and remains unhealed; fear of intimacy; loss of connection with one's heart/with love/with the hearts of others; heart closed from old pain and grief.*

Energetic: Heart chakra; Astral body.

My heart is healed and at peace

ANGEL STAR – (Lesser Stitchwort) *Stellaria graminea*
KEYNOTE: Guiding Light

For remaining clear, defined and aligned with Spirit and True Self during dark and difficult times; knowing one's own path and voice as distinct from the energy of others.

Plant: Lesser Stitchwort is a slender plant of verge-sides, river banks and woods. Its Latin name means 'Grass-like star' and describes both the delicate nature of its stems and leaves, and its clearly defined white flowers. By using the support of other more robust plants, it grows up through them until its constellation of star-like flowers appear as if by magic from the surrounding greenery.

HEALING QUALITIES

Angel Star is the essence for staying clear, defined, and centred in one's own truth, no matter what the circumstances. It facilitates knowing our own light and 'shape' in times when our clarity is threatened by circumstances or energies which confuse us. Like a clear and slender thread of gold in a very dark maze, it helps us to find our way through.

This essence brings definition to Who We Are when we are in a situation where this feels shaken. Often such situations are alchemical fires in which there is potential for a deeper knowledge of Self to be forged. It supports us in retaining our own voice when the voices of others (including voices from the past which echo in one's head) confuse and undermine our confidence and our ability to respond from a simple, gentle and empowered place within. It invites us to step away from entanglement with the energy of the situation or the people in it, remaining clear within one's self. Such situations can feel incredibly dark and frightening, but this essence helps to shed a gentle light into the shadows and illuminate the simple reality. It invites us courageously to walk forward, following that light.

Indications: *Mind full of doubt and uncertainty; feeling overly influenced by the energy of others; entanglement with other people's energy. Uncertainty about where going in life; feeling lost and cut off from intuitive/spiritual guidance. Going through dark times; feelings of despair, darkness, fear, depression; possibly suicidal. Loss of a loved one; facing death - one's own or that of others.*

Energetic:　Root, Solar Plexus and Crown chakras.

I am clear, defined and on my path

ARAGONITE - *Gem Essence*
KEYNOTE: Relationship to the Physical

Feeling warm and secure in one's own body; releasing areas of tension and resistance; knowing one's physical body as home; teaches respect and honouring of the physical body and the Earth.

Gem: Aragonite is a form of calcium carbonate, occurring as a deposit from hot springs.

HEALING QUALITIES

Aragonite supports us in being embodied in a way which feels safe. As a gem, Aragonite has a particular affinity for the spine and extremities; it is said to help release blocks in the energy flow here which may have resulted in a sluggish energy circulatory system (often manifesting in the physical circulatory system). As an essence, Aragonite helps us contact places within us from which energy has withdrawn—from trauma, fear, old memories, etc. It makes it safe to come back by inviting us gently to soften and release these areas so that the energy can flow here once again.

Areas in the body which are tensed and clenched are often indicative of aspects of our being we do not inhabit - here energy is not moving either because there is a vacuum or because it is blocked. Aragonite helps to soothe the body by restoring to consciousness the knowledge that it is safe to inhabit this gift of physicality we have been given. It gently skims off old memories that come up to be released, allowing us to relax and become more fully embodied, feeling the body's warmth and welcome.

As we heal the pain around our own physicality, our own share of the Body Earth, we each contribute to a greater level of healing on a planetary level. This essence invites us to respect and honour not only our own body but the earth on which we live. It helps us move beyond the belief that either of these holds unlimited physical resources, and to re-learn our role as that of a guardian - one who tends and nurtures this physicality that it may thrive.

Indications: *Feeling ungrounded, disconnected from one's body / physicality; sluggishness in physical energy, sense of being blocked; person does not relate to, connect with or engage with body; fear or dislike of body; feeling more comfortable in spiritual/mental realms.*

Energetic: Root, Sacral, Solar Plexus chakras; Circulation; Etheric body; Mental body.

I am relaxed and at ease in my body

BALNAKEIL BAY - *Gem/Environmental Essence*
KEYNOTE: *Self-realisation*

Activation of your True Self; alignment; alchemy; coming into the fullness of you own true nature; realising your potential in this world as a unique individual.

Subject: This essence was made on the white sands of a beautiful secluded bay in the north west of Scotland. The bowl was placed on the shoreline, close to the shimmering turquoise water of the Atlantic as the tide went out; within it a stunning aqua aura crystal, the same deep clean blues and greens as the sea.

HEALING QUALITIES

Balnakeil Bay is for self-realisation: it helps us to come to a place of greater consciousness regarding the totality of who we are and what we have come here to do. The essence helps activate a deep and full awareness of the unique role we have to play in life, and supports us in living this potential. In both senses of the word, then, it helps us 'realise' our true self. As the spiritual teacher, Osho, said: 'You are not accidental. Existence needs you. Without you something will be missing in existence and nobody can replace it.' It is this sense of our entelechy—our essential nature, our guiding principle—to which the essence restores us.

In becoming more deeply aware of our individual nature, we face the reality of our wholeness—our flaws, our beauty, our darkness and our light, our individual challenges and our gifts. Balnakeil Bay helps us comprehend more of *who we are* and all that this entails; and supports us in embracing and accepting the whole of our nature. There is an alchemy that comes from living the true individual potential we each represent in life—and the essence helps us come to this.

It is supportive for anyone who feels thrust in to self-knowledge by life and is struggling with new realisations about themselves; or for those who wish to journey more deeply into an understanding of their place in the whole. It gently illuminates that part of the tapestry of life one particularly pertains to, helping to reveal where one's unique thread lies.

Indications: *Deep processes which are bringing to light new information about oneself; facing one's shadow side; needing to understand more deeply one's gifts and one's individual nature; for bringing greater self-awareness; for dissolving blocks to realising one's true nature and living this fully.*

Energetic: Solar Plexus, Throat and Brow chakras.

I fulfil my true potential

BEE ORCHID - *Ophrys apifera*
KEYNOTE: Individual Path

For those who are creating something exquisite, unique and true in their life and work; brings inspiration, confidence, and support of incredible depth and delicacy on all levels; holds one to this path even when it is solitary and hard; holds the template for what is being created in order that it may be made manifest through you.

Plant: Bee Orchid is found growing on dunes or short turf. Its gorgeous pink and brown velvety heads resemble bees supping at the flower for nectar.

HEALING QUALITIES

Bee Orchid is an essence that supports the manifesting of one's life's work. It reminds you to believe in miracles - the miracles you are capable of creating - in that it supports you in keeping going against impossible odds, against profound inner doubts, and when it feels like there is no external support or interest. It helps you to birth, nourish and bring forth something that you and you alone can create and contribute to the world, to feel its spiritual blueprint within you and remain connected with the vision of it.

This path can at times be extremely difficult, solitary and unrewarding. But it is the path of individuality - what is being created is unique and you are being asked to do that alone so that the energy of it is not diluted or derailed through contact with others. Sometimes it is the very adversity we suffer that gives us the determination to complete.

Bee Orchid helps keep the beauty, the spiritual significance and the depth of what is being produced uppermost. As a plant it is elegant and marvellous. Its vivid bee-like flowers curl around the stem like a spiral staircase. It invites you to keep moving up the staircase, knowing the worth of each step. It is an essence which can support work of epic and life-changing proportions, helping us to manifest our dreams but always in alignment with our spiritual/life truth.

Indications: *Difficulties in connecting with or manifesting one's work in the world; internal/external obstacles; lack of belief/self-doubt; feeling alone and unsupported in this. Needing to connect with the spiritual source of one's work.*

Energetic: Solar Plexus and Brow chakras.

I bring forth that which I am here to create

BIRD'S EYE PRIMROSE - *Primula farinosa*
KEYNOTE: *Inner Vision*

Fosters strong and vital inner vision; clarity to see all perspectives, to look round and take in fully and clearly the truth of your circumstances and to select the way accordingly, in line with your highest vision.

Plant: Bird's Eye Primrose has several small pink flowers, each with a bright golden 'eye', which form a cluster at the top of a single stem. It is found on steep-sided banks, on marshy ground or on limestone, in Northern England and Scotland.

HEALING QUALITIES

Bird's Eye Primrose strengthens our awareness of what it is to See. This essence fosters inner vision and insight into the deeper currents that run through life and the ability to notice, to be awake, alert, and open to sensing in ordinary day-to-day living. In this way it helps us to see how the ordinary is extraordinary and it rekindles our visionary abilities.

The essence facilitates the ability to observe at many different levels at once, to see beyond the material, to discern and sense more than is immediately visible. And it assists in then harmonising and integrating what is seen. With Bird's Eye Primrose we begin to comprehend the wholeness, the patterns, the paths and where they lead, and we see how to tread with greater surety.

Bird's Eye Primrose is also for all those who are developing or who work with a more spiritual or Shamanic way of perceiving the world—who 'walk between two worlds', who may be termed 'seers'. It supports them in integrating and grounding the visions of other worlds with this reality and of living a powerfully *sens*-ual path full of rich perception.

This is an essence which helps us look in all directions and with greater depth, clarity and insight; to become more aware of how we fit most healthfully and beautifully into the tapestry of the whole; and to walk forward with our eyes open and our senses wakefully gathering the information that keeps us shrewd, sure and dancing.

Indications: *Struggling to perceive beyond one's own limited vision of life; tunnel vision; narrow world view. Difficulty in integrating perception that is beyond the ordinary, beyond the five senses. Shamans, seers and healers who 'see' beyond the mundane and need support with this. Wishing to deepen one's visionary abilities.*

Energetic: Sacral, Solar Plexus, Heart and Brow chakras.

I perceive my life with true vision

BLUEBELL - *Hyacinthoides non-scriptus*
KEYNOTE: Trust in Love

Restores us to our purest faith in Love and our trust in the love of those around us; helps us release and move past suspicion and resentment from past mistreatment, to know Love again.

Plant: Bluebell woods are one of the delights of the British countryside. Subtle and beautiful swathes of blue flowers and bright green foliage carpet the ground during May; their bell flowers, usually blue but occasionally white or pink, gracefully bowing on slender stems.

HEALING QUALITIES

Bluebell is a beautiful essence for helping to heal the residues of past hurts and disappointments. It supports us in returning to an innocent belief in Love once more—not from a place of naivety or gullibility—but from innocence tempered with wisdom. Bluebell helps us to learn the lessons of past mistakes and rather than becoming hardened by them, remain open and accepting of their teachings.

It is an essence which supports us in our vulnerability (note the gentle weeping head of the bluebell, its modest and pervasive colour, scent and beauty) and profoundly reminds us of our own beauty and that of other people, when we come from and engage with Love.

Bluebell assists in moving beyond grudges, suspicion, resentment, the inability to forgive. It brings that profound trust that one can feel on falling in love - the ability to see all the good in a person - and tempers this with the wisdom that requires us to accept and communicate with the shadow in ourselves and another in order that a relationship may grow and deepen. It calls on us to be more mature in our love—to move beyond idealism to the expansiveness and compassion of communion.

Indications: *Mistrusting love; resentful, suspicious, guarded; unable to forgive; unable to open to love and intimacy; protecting and defending the heart; inability to be soft and vulnerable with others; past hurts in love – rejection, neglect, betrayal; loss of faith in Love.*

Energetic: Heart and Throat chakras; Emotional body; Astral body.

I trust in love

BOGBEAN - *Menyanthes trifoliata*
KEYNOTE: Healthy Sensitivity

Supports healthy sensitivity and attunement; perceiving clearly, extra-sensory awareness. Protective and stabilizing when 'too sensitive'. Helps bring increased sensitivity when 'too hard'.

Plant: Bogbean grows in streams, bogs and by shallow lakes. Pink buds give way to white star flowers which have bright golden stamen at the centre and are surrounded by a soft cottony fringe.

HEALING QUALITIES

Bogbean essence supports the development of our sensitivity, in ways which are healthy and harmonious. Being 'too sensitive' creates fragility, leaves one feeling exposed and vulnerable to life's knocks and feeling overwhelmed by the needs and feelings of others. Being 'insensitive' involves a sense of hardness, coldness and indifference towards others, and ineptitude when handling other people's moods or our own softer emotions.

Bogbean helps us recover the gift of balanced sensitivity: to become aware of how intimately we are connected to all living things, constantly picking up signals from the collective consciousness, and to help us as we distil this as part of our own unique experience. This process is an inherent part of being human but our ability to attune to this and flow with it productively is a life-skill. For practitioners in particular, this is a very useful essence. It helps us to sense the needs and feelings of others but not be overwhelmed or driven by them; instead balancing this insight with compassion for and protection of our own emotions. It helps us put out 'feelers'; to use our extra sensory perception; to become more attuned to the world around us in ways which are in harmony with the level of insight we are able to assimilate. It also supports the integrity of our aura, protecting the fine nerve-like filaments of our energy-body that are the means by which we interact with the world around us.

Using the gift of healthy sensitivity opens up our ability to read life's terrain more skilfully, to understand the role of the body as subtle interface, and to respond from a place of greater compassion and awareness.

Indications: *Overly sensitive; absorbing the emotions and thoughts of other people/ having to put on a cold, hard 'front' to protect a nature of great sensitivity. To help in sensing the lie of the land in one's life; attuning deeply to the information our senses provide.*

Energetic: Sacral, Solar Plexus, Brow and Crown chakras; connection with our extra-sensory abilities; auric field.

I am highly sensitive and attuned

BUTTERFLY ORCHID - *Platanthera bifolia*
KEYNOTE: *Healing Consciousness*

Cleansing, aligning, reinforcing one's healing energy at every level. Opening to channelling pure healing energy from Spirit; being a conduit of incredible clarity and strength. Removing internal blocks to being a healer.

Plant: Butterfly Orchid is one of our more unusual orchids in Britain. It is white touched with green, lightly fragranced like honey, and often grows in colonies. There is a Greater and Lesser Butterfly Orchid. The essence was made from the more delicate Lesser Butterfly Orchid.

HEALING QUALITIES

Butterfly Orchid is one of the most beautiful flowers I have worked with. Incredibly refined, elegant, graceful and delicate, it has a most wondrous energy. Being with this flower as I made the essence felt like being in the presence of an angel—it feels celestial, compassionate, gentle and deeply healing.

This essence is for healers. It helps in channelling pure healing energy—whether in bodywork, spoken consultations, teaching, meditation, or any other form of healing. It ensures that the energy we draw on for healing is not our own, but comes from Spirit—in this way it protects us from expending all our energy by giving this away to clients, and it protects clients by ensuring that the source we come from is pure.

Butterfly Orchid helps clear any obstructions to this channelling. If we are to be conduits, 'hollow reeds' for the healing energy of the Universe, then our own blocks need first to be addressed. It leads one through that process with great care, cleansing and aligning our subtle energy-matrix. Its other gift is in the gentle, feminine and compassionate energy it helps us to connect with. It helps soften the energy we bring through and send ou,t and supports increasingly strong and pure levels of healing energy.

Indications: *Difficulty channelling healing energy for self and others; energy feeling sluggish/dirty/tainted; blocked energy within the energy-bodies, chakras or pathways; tendency to use own energy in bodywork or healing, rather than bringing in Spiritual energy; healing energy feeling too powerful or overwhelming for clients; learning to become a safe channel.*

Energetic: Crown chakra; central axis of energy running through the core of the spine and body, uniting heavenly and earthly forces; Etheric Template body; Celestial body; Ketheric Template body.

I am filled with healing consciousness

CHICKWEED WINTERGREEN - *Trientalis europaea*
KEYNOTE: *Compassion and Forgiveness*

Absolves and purifies; for when we have learnt things the hard way, through difficult experiences, where there is shame and guilt; clears the heart of negative residue; brings tolerance and healthy remorse.

Plant: Chickweed Wintergreen is a handsome perennial found amongst the undergrowth on forest floors (especially pine woods). Pearly white flowers sit atop a whorl of leaves on a single slender stem.

HEALING QUALITIES

Chickweed Wintergreen has beautiful white star-like flowers whose pearlescent petals shimmer when they catch the light. As an essence, Chickweed Wintergreen wipes the slate clean: it absolves and purifies feelings of guilt and shame.

This is an essence which touches places within us which we are least comfortable revealing to others—places where we hold old pains regarding transgressions we or other people have made which have left us scarred in some way. Regardless of the extent of these experiences and memories in reality, it is the hold they evince over us now which makes them significant. Where they trigger feelings of pain, shame and guilt, this indicates areas within us which remain unresolved and unhealed. Such memories and experiences take energy from us, undermining that deeper sense of our and other people's innocence.

Chickweed Wintergreen works with incredible gentleness to help us release and heal these areas of our psyche and being. When we stay locked in a pattern of guilt and denial, shunning our shadow self and experiences, we do not reach the next part of the cycle—to feel remorse and grief and learn the healing lessons of the situation. The essence brings the internal support to do this. It acts as a welcome balm, restoring us to parts of ourselves and our lives which may have felt monstrous, disgusting, deeply shameful, or just simply uncomfortable. It teaches us to see these anew, to hold them with compassion and composure, and to learn to look into the face of our own pain without judgement. In this way we are able to come to a place of truly tolerating and forgiving ourselves and others.

Indications: *Feelings of shame, guilt and unease; lack of remorse; harsh judgement of one's own 'sins' / those of others; inability to heal and move on from negative experiences; feeling tainted by past experiences.*

Energetic: Sacral, Solar Plexus and Crown chakras; Karmic patterns; (Etheric Template body).

I am innocent and pure

COBWEB HOUSELEEK - *Sempervivum arachnoideum*
KEYNOTE: Harnessing Strength

Connection with deeper levels of inner resources and endurance during lean times; breaking through to new levels of maturity, strength and vitality; finding within ourselves unplumbed depths of richness and resourcefulness.

Plant: Cobweb Houseleek grows on rocky outcrops in dry, warm climates. Often it seems to have hardly any soil to grow in. It looks like a miniature fiery tree and its colour is quite startlingly vivid in the landscape.

HEALING QUALITIES

This essence helps us to find deep sources of strength, endurance, vitality and resourcefulness within ourselves. Cobweb Houseleek invites us to know and harness our own stamina. It is particularly useful for times when support from others may be lacking and we may feel as if we have to endure a great deal without much respite. Rather than be defeated by the situation, Cobweb Houseleek helps us to go more deeply within to find resources we do not even know we have, to uncover new levels of strength, and to come through with greater levels of clarity and brightness.

The essence is very supportive and yet—in spite of its ability to help us dig deep—it is also very light. As a flower it grows on rocky outcrops and its roots are shallow—it sits lightly on hard ground and thrives there, a strong sturdy little plant with a bright red flaming star-flower. It reminds us of this quality in ourselves—to hold the situation lightly, to dance through, to feel our energy and vitality increased by it rather than depleted, to comprehend its gift of healing and health, and let go of the fears and difficulties that would block this.

Cobweb Houseleek is therefore one of the main essences for harnessing physical vitality and strengthening our health through increasing our energetic stamina. With this reservoir of strength we are ready to face and go through lean times, knowing how to care for and tend to our well-being as we do so, knowing how to get the most from our resources and reserves, learning to open to the possibility that we may come out stronger than we went in.

Indications: *Enduring times which challenge one on all levels; feeling stretched and pulled beyond one's limits; overwhelmed, despairing, feeling one hasn't the resources to meet this; feeling one's stamina is ebbing and reserves are running low; knowing one has to dig deeper to get through.*

Energetic: Root, Sacral, Solar Plexus and Crown chakras.

I harness deep resources of vitality and strength

DARK RED HELLEBORINE - *Epipactis atrorubens*
KEYNOTE: *Retrieving Information*

Helps reveal and restore information and knowledge within us that we need to remember at this time in order to move forward; uncovering deep knowledge, hidden abilities; engaging with the mysterious and sacred; key to release.

Plant: Dark Red Helleborine can be found in the deep crevices of limestone paving. It often has to grow quite tall to reach the light beyond these dark grikes but this very environment is both mineral-rich and sustaining for it.

HEALING QUALITIES

Dark Red Helleborine is an incredible looking plant: deep claret-red flowers with gold at the centre adorn its long slender stem, their bell-like heads bowed as if to keep secret that which lies within. This is an essence which draws us towards and evokes in us an awareness of the mystical and sacred in life. Its energy is feminine, potent and rich, inviting us to delve in to this same energy in us; to enter and explore the deeper mysteries of life and uncover new and wondrous ways of looking at, being with, and comprehending it.

The essence helps us gain insight into how we might best reach for and remember hidden skills and knowledge that we need to access now, in order to move forward. Where one feels unable to access the deeper mystery and sacredness of an area of one's life - or where one feels stuck and unable to find the keys that are needed to bring release from a particular situation - it supports you in uncovering and 'reading' the answers that are already there in your life.

At a deeper level, the essence helps us to come to knowledge that is normally reached through profound spiritual practice and experiences. It stirs deep waters within us - resonating with our sexual kundalini energy; our capacity to engage with and co-create with Life; and our awareness of how the mystical and sacred pertain directly to us. It helps us gently embrace and know these energies as they currently relate to us, discovering and comprehending something of their depths, and understanding their potential for bringing us to a richer and more profound connection with the mysterious nature of Life.

Indications: *Loss of connection with deeper mystery of Life; lack of connection with one's creative power/sexual energies/spiritual potency; feeling as if latent skills lie just out of reach; fear of reaching deeper and connecting more profoundly with the Life-force within oneself and within all of creation; lack of deep creative sustenance and soul connection.*

Energetic: (Root), Sacral, Brow and Crown chakras; Kundalini energy.

I open to the mystery and sacredness of life

ENGLISH BEARSFOOT - *Helleborus foetidus*
KEYNOTE: Heart Cleanser

Cleanses the heart of negativity; removes dark energy. Spring-cleans the heart. Rejuvenates, revitalises, reconstitutes the heart's divine energetic structure. Releases negativity that pollutes the heart.

Plant: English Bearsfoot has dark evergreen glossy leaves and stunning light green flowers. A magenta line delineates each petal; an abundance of pale stamens cluster at the mouth of each flower.

HEALING QUALITIES

English Bearsfoot, like other members of the hellebore family, grows and flowers in the depth of winter. Its vivid green foliage and flowers stand out starkly against the dark loamy soil of these fallow months when the surrounding undergrowth has died back and there is very little colour or brightness to be seen.

As an essence, English Bearsfoot cleanses the heart-energy of negativity and taint. Its radiant green healing energy is rejuvenating, uplifting and illuminating. It works gently and deeply to clear blocks, taints and darkness which prevent the heart flourishing fully and joyously. Such darkness can go very deep, even being inherited or karmic; or it can be much more superficial and acute, perhaps as the result of a difficult time that a person is going through. There is the sense that a shadow has been cast over the joyous energy of the heart and one is not able to reach out to dance with Life. There may be physical symptoms in the heart which accompany this state. There is a feeling of one's heart being weighed down, overshadowed, or in darkness; and it may feel compromised, divided or under pressure.

English Bearsfoot helps to clear and clarify the heart's direction, restore balance, reconnect us with the natural vitality and vivacity of the heart, and support us in going out into the world with our hearts strong, vibrant and open. It renews, resolves and lightens the heart. At a deeper level, it goes to the very roots of any darkness that may affect the heart, to transcend and transmute this. It removes all taint of negativity and brings clean, strong, bright spring energy. As such it is an essence of hope, joy and renewal.

Indications: *Darkness, depression, morbid outlook, lack of joy; seeing the world darkly, without trust or hope; closed and negative heart; unable to sit comfortably in the heart; not liking oneself; feeling one's heart is not 'light'.*

Energetic: Root, Heart and Crown chakras; Karmic patterns; Etheric body; Celestial body.

My heart is cleansed of all negativity

FLY ORCHID - *Ophrys insectifera*
KEYNOTE: Into the Dark

Transmuting dark areas of our life and being into that which is rich and potent. Learning our deepest hardest lessons, turning them into gold. Releasing dark clots of consciousness, negativity, and 'dis-ease'. Befriending the dark as that which is rich, fertile and one of our greatest resources.

Plant: Fly Orchid is found on lime-rich soils. These are slight and slender plants, easily overlooked - but their dark insect-like flowers are dramatic when one gets closer.

HEALING QUALITIES

Fly Orchid is an essence which helps us to embrace and befriend the dark. Rather than seeing the shadow side of life as something to shun, shut ourselves off from, or be afraid of—it is like an incredible nutrient-rich compost that helps us grow into our true 'genius' in a way that nothing else can. When we face, accept and work with that which we fear, this ultimately restores that area to us in strength—something that we can rely on, that helps us move beyond previous limitations, that increases our confidence, and that helps us meet life more fully.

For dark obstructive 'clots' of consciousness that stop us from being aligned with our true stream of consciousness—that which comes pure, clean and vital from Spirit—this essence helps us to transmute these clots into gems of richness and depth. A person may be suffering intensely and be in a very dark place of depression and despair, even suicidal. However, they are so close to transforming this darkness into something very rich.

Fly Orchid works well with English Bearsfoot where the darkness is in the mind and consciousness, and in the heart of the person. It also works very well with Butterfly Orchid: as Butterfly Orchid helps one to receive powerful healing light through one's entire energy network, Fly Orchid helps us to embrace and work with that which is dark. In Shamanic work, the dark of the earth is what the Shaman journeys to in order to find rich answers and to communicate with deep areas of the unconscious. Fly Orchid assists this process and helps us to understand that there is nothing to fear in the shadows.

Indications: *Dark thoughts and feelings; fear of the dark in oneself and others; facing one's shadow side; obstructed by dark energies in oneself or one's life; suicidal thoughts – feeling despair and no light or hope.*

Energetic: Root, Sacral, Brow and Crown chakras; Karmic patterns; Mental body; Celestial body.

I embrace the darkness and richness within

FRAGRANT ORCHID – *Gymnadenia conopsea*
KEYNOTE: *Group Harmony*

Harmonious group relationships; raising energy of group to resonate in accord with higher purpose in being together. Attuning to the balance point of the group's energy; harmonious and sensitive connection. Balance of group energy with individual energy. Transmuting negative group energy.

Plant: Fragrant Orchid grows on lime-rich soils, often in communities. The single spike, dense with lightly scented pink flowers, tops a single stem.

HEALING QUALITIES

Fragrant Orchid is a harmonious and graceful flower, elegant and unifying in its energy. As an essence it enables us to unify and harmonise with the higher group consciousness of those we are in community with (our family, friends, work colleagues, people we are thrown together with at significant times) and to become aware of our deeper purpose in coming together. It does not cause us to surrender our individuality and awareness; rather we become cognisant of the higher purpose of the groups we are in and as such become more able to set aside any egoistic needs we have which may be disrupting or standing in the way of the meeting of our higher selves.

All meetings are sacred, be they a fleeting smile from a stranger or the long-term relationships of family and friends. We never meet simply another person. We meet our own Self staring back at us in the beautiful, perfectly imperfect and wondrous form of another individual's living breathing presence. On opening to the gifts this awareness brings we learn what an exquisite boon and blessing is bestowed on us in all our daily encounters, for we are meeting as Spirit in human form.

The essence is particularly appropriate where we are struggling with a specific group (familial or social) and cannot find our place of harmony within it, how we fit together or how as a group we can flow. The essence supports us in coming to consciousness regarding our higher purpose in being with these specific people at this time. As we come into accord with them, we move beyond negativity, doubt, boredom or conflict, and the balance that ensues is both beautiful and meaningful - far beyond what we might have expected.

Indications: *Disunity in groups; unable to comprehend the higher purpose of a relationship; feeling the odd-one-out; strife, conflict and lack of accord; times of dissonance in a group; fear of being overpowered by group energy.*

Energetic: Sacral, Solar Plexus, Heart and Brow chakras; Astral body; Celestial body.

As a group we are harmoniously attuned

GLOBEFLOWER - *Trollius europaeus*
KEYNOTE: Inter-relating

Lifts us beyond a limited world-view; for seeing the bigger picture, understanding how everything inter-relates with everything else; true 'global consciousness'; responsibility for our place and part in the whole—the whole Self, the whole of Life.

Plant: Globeflower grows beside rivers and streams from late spring through to summer, its buoyant golden orbs nodding merrily in the breeze.

HEALING QUALITIES

Globeflower essence helps us comprehend Wholeness - our wholeness as an individual; the wholeness of our life; and the wholeness of all Life. Through the insights it affords, we begin to understand that we play a vital part in constantly and inevitably interacting with, changing and contributing to the whole. It is an essence that brings comfort, for we see more clearly the intricate matrix of life that surrounds and supports us; and it helps us understand our creative responsibility, for nothing can be done in isolation without sending ripples.

Globeflower teaches us something germane to our times - the remembrance that we are all in the same Dream and all aspects of the same living organism. We are reliant on and responsible for each other. We are bound to, supported by and nestled in the completeness of Creation. All is joined, all is connected. What I do touches me, you, Life.

This is an essence which helps us with this concept. It enables us to feel at ease in our own being, at the centre of the Whole, rather than feeling overwhelmed and immobilized by this level of responsibility. We have extraordinary power and gifts at our disposal; for where we begin, where we feel, think and act, so shall we walk. We meet within Life that which we conceive of within ourselves. In our creative reconnection with that which feels whole, good, wholesome within, we meet this externally.

With continuing maturity Globeflower assists us in going further: it invites us to apply this beyond ourselves, to think wholistically about the macrocosm, the people and planet, understanding our potential to support the earth we inhabit from a place of strength, peace and care.

Indications: *Believing one is separate and different; disconnection from community/world/times; acting without awareness of the Whole; difficulty understanding the ripples of one's actions; issues of self-responsibility and self-love; comprehending the wider significance of one's existence.*

Energetic: Solar Plexus, Heart and Throat chakras.

I accept my place and part in the whole

GOLDEN LIGHT - *Environmental Essence*
KEYNOTE: Dancing Forward

Reconnects us with our playfulness and with our dreams; for manifesting 'what happens next' in the life we are creating; keeping hold of our dreams, looking forward to the future; clarity, abundance, play; helps us to keep imagining a rich and beautiful life into fruition.

Subject: Golden Light is an environmental essence, made late one afternoon in the mountains of Cumbria when the land was covered in snow. The low winter sun had turned the white valley golden and a polar maritime wind danced and stirred through the environment.

HEALING QUALITIES

Golden Light essence enables us to align with the spiritual connection that brings appropriate abundance into our future. It is an essence of intense and invigorating clarity and play.

This essence calls on us to play and dream, to dare and imagine. It reminds us to laugh, to open to light and happiness, to experience, to delight and to revel in Life. It is from this place that we are most able to create - spontaneously, abundantly and fruitfully. It helps us to shed our heaviness and our sorrow, our caution and our fearfulness. And it lets us dance into transition without being aware that we are doing it.

Golden Light encourages us to let go and return to a place of childlike trust where we can dream a good dream for our futures and hold it in our mind like stars in the night sky – magical, sacred and blessed.

Indications: *Lack of hope for the future; feeling of powerlessness concerning future events; lack of confidence in creating the life of one's dreams; struggling to take the reins and direct the course of one's life. Children and adults who do not or cannot play; lack of spontaneity; feelings of heaviness and hopelessness; lost or stifled dreams for a promising life.*

Energetic: Solar Plexus and Crown chakras; Astral body; Celestial body; Ketheric Template body.

I dance forward into a joyful future

GRANDFATHER PINE - *Pinus sylvestris*
KEYNOTE: *Empowered Male*

Empowered male: grand; formidable; impregnable; deep and gentle wisdom. Both Grandfather Pine and Grandmother Pine enable us to contact and be strengthened by our ancestral wisdom; for reaching back to our roots, our elders; bringing intricacies of a complex, mature, multi-faceted wisdom; facilitating justice, fairness, good judgement, appropriate action.

Plant: The Caledonian Pines of Scotland are incredibly special. A distinct and separate subspecies of the more common Scot's Pine, they are limited to only a few remaining ancient strongholds. The Grandfather and Grandmother Pines of these essences are true 'elders' – very old pines which tower above the new growth around them.

HEALING QUALITIES

The pine essences in general help wherever one feels shaky, ungrounded, anxious or unsafe. They foster feelings of inner safety, peace, security, being integrated, and being at home within one's self/within a situation. They are essences that enable one to stand tall and firm, in wise and generous ways.

Grandfather Pine brings an impregnable, grand, and formidable energy. This is a towering force and the essence helps connect us with this in ourselves. But it is the towering force of an elder that has been honed and refined by many years of experience and learning, and that is deeply ingrained to the point where strength and wisdom are now intricately combined and have become instinctive. The essence supports one in seeing things from all angles, in being able to plot one's way by taking into account the needs of all, in being centred - a force of strength and compassion on whom others can rely. It releases feelings of shakiness and anxiety and is particularly good to help the young grow tall, straight and strong within, and to help the elderly know the value and strength of their many years of experience.

Indications: *Disconnected from ancestors/family tree, especially on the male side; feeling far away from one's 'roots' in all senses of the word; ungrounded, anxious, unsafe; feeling cut off from one's wisdom and deep knowing; disconnected from one's yang energy.*

Energetic: Root, Heart, Brow and Crown chakras in unity; Etheric body; Yang energy.

I access deep grounding, strength and wisdom

GRANDMOTHER PINE - *Pinus sylvestris*
KEYNOTE: Empowered Female

Empowered female: energy of the matriarch, impressive force, gateway, command. Both Grandmother Pine and Grandfather Pine enable us to contact and be strengthened by our ancestral wisdom; for reaching back to our roots, our elders; bringing intricacies of a complex, mature, multi-faceted wisdom; facilitating justice, fairness, good judgment, appropriate action.

Plant: The Caledonian Pines of Scotland are incredibly special. A distinct and separate subspecies of the more common Scot's Pine, they are limited to only a few remaining ancient strongholds. The Grandfather and Grandmother Pines of these essences are true 'elders' – very old pines which tower above the new growth around them.

HEALING QUALITIES

The pine essences in general help wherever one feels shaky, ungrounded, anxious or unsafe. They foster feelings of inner safety, peace, security, being integrated, and being at home within one's self/within a situation. They are essences that enable one to stand tall and firm, in wise and generous ways.

Grandmother Pine offers rounded, warm, embracing, 'wise woman' energy: the energy of the matriarch—protective, commanding, forceful. This essence teaches us to open up to this wisdom within, to open to teachings that we might only be able to hear and accept from a wise elder woman of our 'tribe', from our own ancestral knowing. This is often survival wisdom—teachings which will help us go forward more adeptly, less clumsily, returning our feet to safe ground. The teachings are not always easy to follow; the illumination of consciousness may bring some uncomfortable awareness. But the essence can provide a catalyst to release us from areas of stubbornness, blindness and wilfulness, and to help us to find a more rounded, embracing attitude.

Indications: *Disconnected from ancestors/family tree, especially on the female side; feeling far away from one's 'roots' in all senses of the word; ungrounded, anxious, unsafe; feeling cut off from one's wisdom and deep knowing; disconnected from one's yin energy.*

Energetic: Root, Heart, Brow and Crown chakras in unity; Etheric body; Yin energy.

*I open to the deep wisdom of
the Feminine*

GRAND QUINTILE - *Gem/Astrological Essence*
KEYNOTE: Dissolving Defences

Moving beyond states of difference and separateness; letting inner defences relax into and merge with Love; stepping towards Oneness whilst still maintaining healthy boundaries and the ability to discern; being guided by beautiful, compassionate heart-energy.

Subject: This essence was made during the astrological Harmonic Concordance of October 2004. The gems were arranged to mirror the formation of the five planets in the sky – the quintile.

HEALING QUALITIES

Grand Quintile is a gem, astrological and environmental essence combined. As such it is both potent and supportive. It provides a catalyst for dissolving barriers which are inappropriate, defensive and outdated. It does this by inviting us to return to a place where all communication is of the Heart and Spirit. It helps us go beyond the barriers of the physical world - of time, space, culture, language - and return to the reality of energy, which is much more pervasive, fluid, permeable and malleable. It is a place where nothing is set in stone; Creation is unfolding in myriad ways on myriad levels.

Grand Quintile enables us to see the nature of our own limitations - of the boundaries we place around ourselves, the walls and defences - and to expand beyond them. It is an essence for leaving behind outmoded behaviours and ways of being, especially where these come from fear and reaction. Instead it invites us to rest in the eternal space of the Heart and feel the fluidity of all Life as it moves in and through us in this present moment. In this space we are naturally protected and naturally respond from a place of universal truth and appropriateness. Here we merge into Oneness whilst staying absolutely clear and defined in who we are. Here it is possible to say no and state our needs without losing our compassion for others. Here it is possible to dissolve barriers whilst still retaining form and individuality.

This essence helps update our system to let in more light and to enable us to ascend to a higher level of conscious awareness and compassion. It is an essence of surrendering and of empowerment.

Indications: *Chronic feelings of defensiveness; fear of losing one's individuality if one surrenders to the Oneness; inability to conceive of and merge with the unity of all things; tendency towards unhealthy, rigid or ineffective boundaries in work, relationships, life; scepticism and fear of spirituality.*

Energetic: Heart, Throat and Crown chakras; Astral body; Celestial body.

I move from separateness to Oneness

GRASS OF PARNASSUS - *Parnassia palustris*
KEYNOTE: Celebrating Your Light

Knowing, owning, celebrating your own individual, exquisite and pure inner light; living your beautiful nature with truth and modesty; relinquishing habits of giving light away/denying it; standing in the light of Who You Are.

Plant: Grass of Parnassus grows in communities on boggy ground, usually in the mountains. This essence was made in the French Alps where the flowers are particularly large and more luminous. The petals seem to have been delicately and exquisitely veined by an artist. As with Herb Paris, the incredible symmetrical patterns, echoed in the stamen and modified stamen show this to be a plant for balance and alignment.

HEALING QUALITIES

This essence strengthens your ability to stand in your full power without feeling apologetic, embarrassed or unworthy, and without imposing this power on others. It helps us perceive our innate beauty and purity, gently reminding us of this, whatever else we may have come to believe about ourselves.

The chalice-like flower holds and reflects the light. It grows on a single stem rising up through a heart-shaped leaf. As an essence it brings us to an awareness of the Light that pervades all Creation, including ourselves; an awareness we reach through our own heart. It helps us contain our own light and strength—not leaking away our power, light, or beauty through feelings of unworthiness. Rather than giving away that which is integral to us, it helps us to strengthen and maintain it.

Many people fear to shine their light, to be fully all they can be, to stand in the centre of their own magnificence - modest yet powerful. As Marianne Williamson famously wrote: 'Our deepest fear is not that we are inadequate. Our deepest fear is that we are powerful beyond measure. It is our light, not our darkness, that most frightens us.'

Grass of Parnassus helps us to feel safe in our power and inner beauty, to shine our light with grace and modesty, comfortable with the truth of our own majesty.

Indications: *Giving away one's power and light; self-sabotage; self-negating; uncomfortable with / unaware of / un-acknowledging of one's beauty and worth; inability to stand in one's own power consistently; arrogance or fear around matters of personal power and the power of others.*

Energetic: (Root and Sacral chakras); Solar Plexus and Crown chakras; Auric field; Celestial body.

I embrace my power and light

GREATER CUCKOOFLOWER – *Cardamine raphanifolia*
KEYNOTE: Loving Intimacy

Friendship, companionship, community, communion with others. Meeting others with love; forging strong bonds of friendship and trust. Social ease and confidence. Mutual responsibility.

Plant: This striking plant is the cousin of our common Lady's Smock or Cuckooflower. Greater Cuckooflower grows in woods, beside running water or in marshy shaded areas. It is a robust buoyant perennial with gorgeous deep pink flowers.

HEALING QUALITIES

Greater Cuckooflower essence helps engender and strengthen feelings of intimacy, companionship and friendship. Supportive for all aspects of relating, it helps one to feel at ease with the company of others; to trust; to open up; to be willing to engage and take responsibility; and to enjoy and take pleasure in one's relationships. Its energy creates feelings of trust, intimacy, openness, playfulness and balance. Heart-warming and joyful, it helps us to revel in the pleasure of being with others and assists us in being present and aware so that we can dance in the moment of interaction with humour and lightness.

Greater Cuckooflower is an essence for anyone who struggles with socialising, friendship, relationships, and community. This may be through shyness and a lack of ease in the company of others, or it may be because others find them difficult or awkward to be around and so tend to avoid them.

For people who feel alone and outside, it helps one move towards creating enduring, mutually-supportive and enjoyable relationships with others. And it is also good for anyone who wants to strengthen their connections further and deepen their ability to find support, love and pleasure in the company of others. A lovely essence to spray around at parties or communal gatherings—it creates openness, receptivity, and willingness to engage.

Indications: *Lonely, separate, outside things; difficulty in making friends; struggling with intimacy and opening up to others; shyness, awkwardness; fear of being in groups / with other people; relationships which are stilted, unresponsive, lacking play and fellowship; difficulty in social situations.*

Energetic: (Sacral chakra), Solar Plexus and Heart chakras.

I embrace friendship and intimacy

HAWTHORN BERRIES - *Crataegus monogyna*
KEYNOTE: Fruition

Fruition, receiving the fruits of your labours; receiving your heart's desire; letting go of suffering and lack; finding the heart's home; coming into your own, your inheritance, your spiritual legacy.

Plant: Hawthorn Berries are used herbally as a heart tonic to help balance the rhythms of the heart. Their bright red berries can be seen flourishing on Hawthorn trees in the Autumn where they make rich contrast with their glossy green leaves.

HEALING QUALITIES

Hawthorn Berries helps us to receive what our heart desires, to make room for this within, and to remain firmly rooted and open-armed when it comes to accepting it. It is useful for anyone who struggles in this area - who finds it hard to recognize, receive or hold onto abundance. The essence gently releases the internal resistance we may have to receiving our true worth by increasing our awareness and insight, realigning our internal energy system to allow the flow, the give and take, of abundance. It strengthens the heart - its rhythm, beauty, dreams - to give it good grounding from which to flourish; it encourages us to seek the 'food' our heart truly needs (in all senses of the word) in order to blossom and bloom in strength and wholeness.

Life constantly offers us its gifts and grace. This essence helps us to receive and welcome these and let them nourish us - letting go of expectation, receiving what is and trusting the path of wholeness.

At a deeper level it invites us to come fully into our own, to accept our inheritance, to become comfortable with receiving what we need from this earth without plundering it or denying others, to be fully attuned to our desires so that the life we live can be desirable for us. When we allow ourselves to become full we are able to share our good fortune with others. This essence increases our capacity for receiving life's gifts of grace, for drawing them towards us without needing to push them away or sabotage our success.

Indications: *Despair at attaining one's heart's desire; inability to receive – from others / the universe; overly-identified with suffering, lack, poverty, unhappiness; sundered from one's desires; sabotaging abundant and joyous opportunities.*

Energetic: Heart and Throat chakras.

I fully receive the fruits of my labours

HAWTHORN BLOSSOM - *Crataegus monogyna*
KEYNOTE: Gifts and Blessings

For truly accepting and being at one with your life as it is; counting gifts and blessings; ceasing to yearn and hanker for what is not or what might have been; settling into the everyday and working with the richness of What Is.

Plant: This essence was made in the mountains of the Lake District during a year when the Hawthorn blossom was so prolific it seemed as if the valleys were full of snow trees.

HEALING QUALITIES

This essence assists us in accepting and embracing what is, where we are in our lives, what we have - accepting our lot and seeing within it the enormous gifts it holds for us. Hawthorn Blossom provides a gentle catalyst for coming away from patterns of dissatisfaction, complaining, feelings of lack, feelings of being 'hard-done-to'. It helps us fully to embrace the here and now, rather than struggle against it.

For the striving, yearning and expectation that takes one out of the bounty of what is and has us looking only at what is not, Hawthorn Blossom realigns our perspective and sharpens our insight. It invites us to remember the abundance and harmony that exists all around us; where potentially, 'Everything is exactly as it needs to be, all I need is here and everything is perfect.' With this we are profoundly empowered to realise the potential and wonder of what Life has already placed before us – in it are the seeds of everything we wish to create.

The essence helps us truly to count our blessings and to experience domestic harmony by knowing the worth of what is often right under our noses. It helps us to weave a cloth of gold from the gifts that we have in the present.

At a deeper level it assists us in letting go of the need for stimulus, instant gratification, the desires of a materialistic society - to become aware of the real, nourishing, readily available riches of Life; those which truly satisfy our soul.

Indications: *Unhappy with one's lot in life; wishing for more; disgruntled. Feeling the 'grass is greener' somewhere else. Not appreciating the gifts and blessings of your life as it is. Failing to see, rejoice in and wield the resources in front of you. Yearning, hankering, pining for what is not.*

Energetic: Solar Plexus, Heart, Throat and Crown chakras; Emotional body.

I gratefully receive the gifts I have in my life

HERB PARIS – *Paris quadrifolia*
KEYNOTE: *Structural Integrity*

Establishing balance, cohesion and structural integrity in the physical body; awareness of functions, systems and structures of our body / being/ life; working with the systems that support us internally and externally.

Plant: A whorl of four large leaves sits below the striking lime green flower of Herb Paris. The plant grows in woodlands on lime in dense colonies.

HEALING QUALITIES

Herb Paris is an essence of symmetry and balance, cohesion and order; of things being in their rightful place. The vivid green of its flower indicates its ability to connect us with our healing force and power; the cosmic quality of the star and its cumulative layers of sepals, stamens and styles, indicate the complex and systemic ability of the essence to touch the various levels of our own energy structure and help balance and harmonise these.

The essence works at a pre-physical level. It touches and realigns us with those layers of our subtle energy-anatomy which are to do with our structural blueprints; the balanced and harmonious precursor to our physical form.

Maintaining the harmony between these, the clear flow and communication, Herb Paris enables us to live our cosmic order, our deeper structure and ultimate fluidity. It is an essence to raise us beyond our earthly sense of our form as it appears to present to us now with all its flaws and limitations. It raises us beyond our preoccupations with our body's 'problems' or discomfort, and it helps us understand instead how the energetic space we occupy is divinely imbued and has an integrated order. It invites us to reach back to these energetic roots which anchor us in the phenomenally intricate and ordered web of Life.

On a practical level, Herb Paris is for use where there is illness and dysfunction; where the systems of one's body are ill-at-ease and uncoordinated; where the overall structure of the body as a whole entity needs support and cohesion. This essence helps us feel our way back to our true form, our pre-physical harmony; and bring this through at a cellular level, re-establishing harmony and integrity of structure.

Indications: *Illness, discomfort, dis-ease; energetic / structural / systemic imbalances. Lack of harmony, balance and cohesion within one's energy-bodies, physicality, between systems of the body and being.*

Energetic: Root, Solar Plexus, Heart and Crown chakras; Etheric body; Etheric Template body; Bodily Systems and their structural integrity; Cellular stability.

The foundations of my health are strong

LADY'S SLIPPER ORCHID – *Cypripedium calceolus*
KEYNOTE: *Healthy Vitality*

For living the knowledge that we can heal; reconnecting with our healing potential; true vitality; what healing means for us. Overcoming obstacles and dissolving boundaries to true healing.

Plant: A large yellow pouch makes up the flower of the rare Lady's Slipper Orchid, surrounded by gracefully spreading maroon petals and sepals.

HEALING QUALITIES

Lady's Slipper Orchid restores us to full knowledge of and belief in our ability to heal. As a plant it is vital and potent. As an essence it imparts certainty and dynamism to us, enabling us to engage with our innate wholeness and the undeniable existence of this even in times of illness.

The essence enables us to know and live the gift of vitality by reconnecting us with our inner healing force - in this we are offered an incredible balm for the spirit and insight for the mind. It reminds us that we can heal anything and have within the knowledge to do this. This knowledge can mobilise us to move forward with our healing journey - whether this is to surrender to the gifts of an illness or shake off the ties of sickness, depending on our circumstances.

In any situation where there is lack of hope, strength and trust that things can and will get better. Where we are out our lowest ebb and do not believe in the dynamic power of our life-force (the vitality within us that will see us through), Lady's Slipper Orchid re-establishes our connection with this inner potency. It reaffirms that we have the strength and certainty within to continue; and that healing is possible, though the shape and feel of it may currently be beyond our ken. It allows us to open to the possibility that we may be on a journey that is mysterious, profound and holy, and to be led by our inner knowing rather than external perceptions and mental concepts. Illness is the body changing; sickness is an internal environment of defeat and hopelessness. Following these changes overcomes sickness and allows us to be seeded in the vital complexity of that which is transmuting at our core.

Indications: *Loss of belief in ability to heal. Handing over power of healing to external authorities. Overwhelmed by the demands of one's healing path. Fearing external manifestations of disease rather than staying with the internal process of transformation.*

Energetic: Root, Solar Plexus, Brow and Crown chakras; Etheric body.

I harness my healing vitality

LA MEIJE - *Environmental Essence*
KEYNOTE: *Spiritual Majesty*

Rising up to meet the place within where your spirit soars, connecting with the Absolute, the great I Am; for sitting at the foot of your own sacred mountain and meeting your path and calling; going beyond previously known limits—facing the terror and splendour.

Subject: La Meije is an imposing and majestic mountain in the French Alps in Le Parc National des Ecrins. Here the variety of flora is exceptional. Within the glacier, amazing ice sculptures are created by artists and it is possible to go into the caverns of the glacier to see them and to observe the deep natural crevices below the surface.

HEALING QUALITIES

La Meije is an essence that inspires and holds us when we are facing our true calling. It is supportive when one is looking up at one's own spiritual mountain in life and feeling tiny, vulnerable and not up to the job - when what lies ahead is both awesome and terrifying. It could be manifesting as one's life work, a fundamental shift in direction, or as an inner call to live very differently with much deeper values.

When we look at that path, and look at where we have been, the way back can seem more comfortable, or at least safer, than the path that goes ahead.

La Meije is for when we are in that place of choice—not the little everyday choices—at a real crossroads where we have the chance to enter into a much deeper, richer, more sustaining and more risky connection with Life or where we can stay in a place which is perhaps a little more sleepy and more secure.

La Meije gives us the opportunity to see beyond our fears and see the beauty of where we are. It reminds us our grounding is firm, we are not alone, we only have to reach out our hand to be held in Spirit and guided. It beckons us to risk and trust; to meet this point where Life has issued us with a command, knowing that we will be supported, cradled and sustained in every moment.

Indications: *Fear of moving forward, meeting one's destiny, heeding one's calling. Feeling bound by the apparent safety and security of present circumstances, even though one has outgrown them. Fearful of expanding one's horizons and moving beyond one's comfort zone.*

Energetic: Solar Plexus, Throat, Brow and Crown chakras.

I embrace my path and calling

LE JARDIN DES ALPES - *Environmental Essence*
KEYNOTE: *Reassurance*

For moving within to a space of inner contemplation and meditation; resting, renewing, relaxing; letting go of external demands for a period in order to return to gentleness and compassion within; being present.

Subject: This essence was made one rosy dawn in the mountains in Le Parc National des Ecrins, French Alps. Here mineral-rich flushes enable incredible mountain gardens to thrive. Making this essence in the cold clear dawn was an experience of stillness, contemplation, peace and oneness.

HEALING QUALITIES

This essence is about taking time to rest and renew, to retreat from the demands of external life in order to reconnect with one's internal life, to become more present. It brings a sense of peace and gentleness, of being in a beautiful meadow on a sunny day and resting - letting the sun come into your bones and warm them, letting yourself recharge.

At a deeper level, Le Jardin Des Alpes is for letting go of attachment to external demands, to the needs of others, to the world beyond. It encourages one to trust the life within, the life that is connected to everything else. It reminds us to listen, to stop, to breathe more slowly, to contemplate, to let go of hurrying, to let life slow down with us, to relax. It stimulates us to find renewal in the everyday rather than waiting for some imaginary time in the future when we hope we will stop and be still. It invites us to rest within the moment. And initially this may mean stepping back, breathing deeply, hearing the birds, feeling the sun or the warmth of a fire, returning our body and mind to safety and comfort.

An essence of peace and of gentleness, Le Jardin des Alpes reminds us to renew ourselves, bringing reassurance on every level as we connect with our inner needs for regular care, maintenance and relaxation. It is not enough to rest the body and leave the mind worried, active and preoccupied. It is not enough to switch off the mind and emotions and exhaust the body. Rest involves balancing all areas of one's being in order to restore harmony and order once more.

Indications: *Overwrought, busy, under stress; unable to slow down and come back to stillness; tension, hurriedness; afraid to surrender, switch off and relax; not allowing for ebb and flow of life, of own energy – constantly on the go; does not incorporate time for relaxation and renewal in daily life; physically clumsy and uncoordinated from tiredness.*

Energetic: Root, (Sacral) and Brow chakra; Mental body.

I now rest, rejuvenate and relax

LINDEN BLOSSOM – *Tilia vulgaris*
KEYNOTE: Joyful Heart

Helps to uplift and lighten the heart; joyful heart; spontaneity; balancing and harmonising work and play through lightness and creativity; tenderness and healing where the heart is burdened, weighty and serious.

Plant: Linden Blossom was made into an essence by Beth Tyers in the first years of this millennium. The blossoms of the Linden Tree are a beautiful creamy white, incredibly profuse and with a wonderful heady perfume. They move lightly in the breeze, buoyant and fair.

HEALING QUALITIES

The large and beautiful tree in a wood near Beth Tyers' house had been calling her for some time with its uplifting message. She would often drink the blossoms as tea and go to sit by the tree for comfort and to meditate.

On the morning she made the essence, she was in the field below its branches, just outside the boundary of the wood. She felt extraordinarily blissful and light-hearted. As she sat there, a farmer came in his noisy tractor to take in the crop. She felt both embarrassed and in the way, sitting there meditating in the corner. However, he genially waved to her as he went past and she decided that she would stay, absorbing the message this added dimension brought. It was only later that she realised how much work and play had been the theme running through her musings (and indeed her life) at that time.

Speaking about the essence later, Beth radiated the most delicious bubbly joyful energy – like champagne! Light, sparkly, excited and humbled by the experience, she was glowing with the energy of the Linden Blossom. She felt the essence was a true tonic for the heart and the means to balance spontaneous joyful living and laughter, with productive and creative work - without the weariness and heavy sense of duty so often associated with it.

Linden Blossom helps us to dance into harmony regarding our work, understanding that it is the precious means by which we fulfil our destiny in the world and put forward our creativity; expressing this through playful spontaneity and glad-hearted laughter.

Indications: *Heavy-hearted, particularly around issues of work; loss of balance between work and play; overly serious; weary; forlorn; lacking in joy and spontaneity; heavy and dispirited.*

Energetic: Heart, Crown, Brow and Throat chakras. Also Solar Plexus (secondary).

My heart is light

LUNAR STANDSTILL – *Environmental/Flower/Astrological Essence*
KEYNOTE: Embracing Change

Helps you connect deeply with your intuition; to stay fluid, soft, and responsive during change; catalyst for times when you are stuck or resist change; letting the movement of change course through you, bringing energy, creativity and confidence.

Subject: Lunar Standstill is an environmental, gem and flower essence. It was made on a small tidal island, off one of the remote islands of Orkney. Bordered on one side by the North Sea and on the other by the Atlantic, its small beaches offer one of the few remaining strongholds for the Oyster Plant—a rare ground-hugging plant with thick silvery blue leaves and dozens of diminutive pink and blue flowers. The bowl was left for the night as the high tide cut off this patch of land. It rested on a bed of Oyster Plant, surrounding by two seas, under an enormous full moon, both pulled and anchored by these forces: an essence of moon, flower and tides.

HEALING QUALITIES

Lunar Standstill helps us find our natural rhythm - be this circadian rhythm, sleep pattern, menstrual cycle/menopause—and to find a new rhythm when our old one has been disrupted.

Our rhythm, our flow, and our sense of harmony in our life, are all intricately linked. When this is disturbed through change, or where it has become heavy and stuck in a pattern which no longer serves us, we can feel profoundly affected. This essence helps restore us to our inner sense of how best we may move with these currents, supporting us when we are struggling to find our natural balance in a particular cycle or phase of our journey.

Lunar Standstill invites us to step into the core of the rhythm we are feeling—into its momentum and flow—and connect deeply with our intuitive sense of how it naturally needs to move through us, and how we need to move with it. It is said that it is our resistance to flow that causes us to suffer. This essence helps us go with the tides of change and the natural cycles of life, conscious of the depths shifting and a new cycle beginning.

Indications: *Struggling to accept and flow with change; unable to find one's movement within it; feeling at the mercy of these tides. Disconnected from one's natural rhythms; going against these; struggling to restore them. Menstrual / menopausal difficulties; fear of surrendering to the flow.*

Energetic: Sacral and Throat chakras.

I move and flow with change

MARSH FELWORT – *Swertia perennis*
KEYNOTE: *Applying Your Wisdom*

Bringing own spiritual wisdom and sophistication to everyday life; working with the flow; heeding, sensing, attending to one's inner voice and mastery and applying this practically; spiritual discipline and resolve.

Plant: This dusky plant with flowers of smoky purple and blue hues is found in Alpine regions. The essence was made in the French Alps.

HEALING QUALITIES

Marsh Felwort supports us in practising what we preach, living our spiritual beliefs, applying the teachings of our inner wisdom. It bridges the gap between theory and practice, enabling us consciously to embody our inner knowing so we may live our spiritual wisdom practically, not merely intellectually.

In some ways it is an essence for 'being good at life' in that it helps us to apply and live what we know. It enables us to become conscious of the wisdom we have within which guides us in every moment, and to heed and act from it. Thus it is for the practical application of wisdom. As such it helps us grow more aware of mistakes we keep repeating through not listening to our inner guidance. It invites us to walk our wisdom and go through life with a greater degree of sophistication, no longer ignoring the deeper truth that is within us all.

Marsh Felwort helps us listen within for our true spiritual path and practice, learning what complements and marries with our own essence, having the resolve to protect this practice and carry it through into our everyday living. This is not to say that we must meditate every day in a certain way because we have been told to, yet it presents a constant struggle. Instead, Marsh Felwort helps us find living practices which are conducive to our growth, our deepening contact with our innate wisdom, and our peace. To spend time sitting quietly in a place which feels like a beautiful balm to your spirit, can be a more healing path for some than hours of meditation. Similarly, speaking with love and awareness; making decisions based on one's truth; living peacefully – all are practices which allow us to apply our spirituality and bring it into our lives in enriching and uplifting ways. In this our spirituality becomes our daily reality and succour.

Indications: *Not heeding one's inner wisdom; making mistakes through inability to learn the lessons; incongruity and inconsistency between spiritual beliefs and way one lives one's life.*

Energetic: Throat, Brow and Crown chakras; (Mental Body).

I am guided by my spiritual wisdom

MARSH HELLEBORINE – *Epipactis palustris*
KEYNOTE: *Moving Out Into The World*

Moving out into the world with confidence and ease, especially after periods of retreat or introversion. Finding our way in the world; taking our teaching/knowledge/gifts out to others.

Plant: Marsh Helleborine has striking white and pink flowers which look out in every direction with open wings. It grows in colonies in marshy ground.

HEALING QUALITIES

Marsh Helleborine essence supports us in moving out into the world, especially after a time where our life has been very contained, narrow or restricted. It helps us trust that we can move out; that we can reach for others with our gifts and learning; that we can connect fruitfully with the people, organisations, experiences and situations that we need; and that we can do this lovingly and openly, embracing what we meet.

The essence helps us journey beyond ourselves, stepping over the old boundary lines of our life as it used to be; expanding to touch new horizons and explore new areas. It is an essence that supports us in moving outward from the known self and becoming more than one currently experiences oneself to be. From the combined water and earth elements in which this plant grows – the dark rich sustenance of boggy ground full of nutrients - we are given grounding and emotional equilibrium. With this to stabilize us, we feel safe enough to look beyond the circumference of our 'little' world and move into the unknown.

Marsh Helleborine encapsulates a beautiful, inquisitive, curious energy with which to explore life. For those who have been in retreat; who are naturally shy, introverted or reclusive; or who have been experiencing a time away from the bustle of life and are now ready to return, this essence helps one to emerge in a way which feels safe. It supports us in showing our face to the world and coming out of 'hiding'. It is often the case in such times that we emerge to show more of our deeper self than we have previously revealed (or known). It helps us move beyond fears of releasing ourselves to the unknown, both internal and external, so that we can gently break with the past and move forward into a more expansive way of being.

Indications: *Fear of moving out into the world; wishing to stay hidden and unknown; afraid to shine and to show one's power and gifts to others; fear of being in the public eye; timidity; difficulty in returning to a group/community/society after time spent apart or alone; returning from meditation/retreat.*

Energetic: Sacral, Throat and Crown chakras.

I am moving out into the world

MARSH MARIGOLD – *Caltha palustris*
KEYNOTE: *Mental and Physical Balance*

For learning to balance excessive 'head' energy with the needs of the physical body; coming from a place within where each is given equal voice; keen mental acuity and brightness; where excessive mental activity leads to patterns of physical ill-health and exhaustion.

Plant: Marsh Marigold (or 'kingcup') grows on boggy ground, lighting up whole areas of marshland with its bright golden flowers and glossy green leaves. It flowers from March through to early summer.

HEALING QUALITIES

Marsh Marigold supports strength, clarity and balance in the mental sphere. Where there is a tendency to over-use the mental faculties to the exclusion of other areas of our being, the essence can help us to become aware of this imbalance. Excessive studying, reading, use of one's critical and analytical abilities, debating, etc., can all lead to feeling fatigued and worn out. Marsh Marigold addresses the patterns of imbalance that lead to this, helping us to stay connected with our emotional, spiritual and physical needs so that these are not over-ridden by this 'head-strong' aspect.

It is also supportive where the mental realm feels clouded, doubt-ridden and unsure; where we are unable to come to a clear sense of something, only feeling uncertainty and despair. It is as if, in such times, we cannot get the mind to provide an answer and yet continue to push and push it, sure that the answer must lie there. Marsh Marigold is once again reminding us to come into the balance of all realms; to have the mind sit within the support of heart, body and soul; and to let the answers come bright, strong and clear from all of these aspects working together. It helps us to let go of pushing the mind and thus often pushing and punishing ourselves. These flowers look like beacons of strong golden yellow light; they are bright, optimistic and confident. They invite us to come to this energy within our own mental sphere, finding again our mental vitality and acuity.

Indications: *Living too much in the head; mental fatigue; struggling to come up with answers through rational thought processes; inability to access intuition because of mental turmoil and indecision; doubt and uncertainty; bodily weariness from excessive study; over-intellectualisation; tendency to neglect and devalue the body, emotions, spirit.*

Energetic: Solar Plexus and Crown chakras; Mental body.

I am balanced and clear in mind and body

MONKSHOOD – *Aconitum napellus*
KEYNOTE: Good Medicine

Finding and harnessing own personal 'good medicine' for one's self and one's community; finding abundance, vitality, physical health in the natural world; drawing to self and others that which nurtures, upholds, sustains.

Plant: Monkshood ('wolfsbane', 'leopard's bane') is a tall handsome perennial growing in mountainous areas in the Northern hemisphere. It has racemes of deep blue flowers, each of which looks like a monk's cowl.

HEALING QUALITIES

Monkshood Essence is for seeing where vitality lies and harnessing it for one's own good and the good of one's community. It stirs in us our ability to embrace and protect those things which may be considered our own 'good medicine'—the particular and appropriate nourishment, relationships, livelihood, environment, exercise, ways of being, etc., which support our health and wellbeing. It helps us to discern them, listen for them in any given set of circumstances, and heed them; retaining a healthy awareness of the fact that we are ultimately responsible for ourselves and our own wellbeing. As we develop this awareness we are increasingly able to see beyond the self to the health needs of our community - human, animal, environmental - to understand vitality at a deeper level.

Monkshood helps us to become aware of the patterns which are detrimental to our wellbeing and which do not serve to enhance and nurture our vitality. True vitality and health arise first and foremost from an inner state of balance which is then carried through by thoughts, words and actions into the manifestation of our outer world. We design and create our world to a much greater extent than we realise. This essence helps to bring this more fully into our consciousness and to strengthen our ability to draw to us that which we truly need in order to thrive, in balance with the needs of the environment and others - to sense where health lies and to move towards that which is life-affirming rather than life-denying.

Indications: *Habitually drawn to those things which are not healthy for oneself or one's community; addictions and obsessions; poor choices regarding one's spiritual growth and one's wellbeing on all levels; attracting negative situations and experiences. Inability to create a loving and healing environment for ourselves and others.*

Energetic: Throat and Brow chakras; Mental body.

*I draw to me all I need for health
and happiness*

PINK PURSLANE – *Claytonia sibirica*
KEYNOTE: *Physical Intimacy*

Opening to our sexual and sensual nature at deeper levels. Long-term physical communion with our loved one. Feeling safe in our sexuality. Expressing our love with pleasure and playfulness.

Subject: Pink Purslane grows low to the ground near water. It is seen with pink or white flowers. The essence also contains Rose Quartz, making it both a flower and gem essence.

HEALING QUALITIES

The Pink Purslane has an incredibly soft and tender energy. As an essence it gently eases us into embracing and expressing our sensual nature and our sexuality in ways which are congruent and born from within. It helps us to express our sensuality as a unique celebration of self in and of our relationship with our beloved, thus moving away from the external and often inappropriate or ineffective images of sexual expression we receive from the world around us.

This essence helps us with the everyday love of a long-term relationship, increasing our ability to connect with this deeply so that it becomes more intimate and profound over time. Pink Purslane encourages us to open our senses to our beloved – feeling the needs of our mutual expression; seeking deeper connection, movement, rhythm; and finding new levels of physical-emotional-spiritual conjoining. It supports easeful, joyous sexual and sensual connection and awareness. The flower has a light buoyant dancing quality to it and is graceful yet unpretentious. This is not about rarefied love or emotion – this is down-to-earth, accessible, every-day loving expression which is nourishing and fulfilling.

However resistant a person may be to their sexuality or to being with another person in this way, this essence works lightly and joyfully to help them find their own natural expression of sexuality and sensuality. For people who have suffered sexual abuse or who wish to bring healing to their feelings around sexuality /their own body /union with another – this essence acts as a gentle and intuitive guide. It helps nurture feelings of confidence, intimacy, tenderness and play, and encourages us to meet this in and with our loved one.

Indications: *Discomfort with own sexuality or sexual expression in loved one; feeling disconnected from one's sensual nature; loss of intimacy in long-term relationship; connecting with one's sensuality and sexuality healthfully; playful and joyous expression.*

Energetic: Sacral, (Solar Plexus) and Heart chakras.

I enjoy loving physical intimacy

PRIMROSE – *Primula vulgaris*
KEYNOTE: Good Love

Loving with all the boundlessness of one's being whilst accepting the boundaries; appropriate love; letting go of giving or receiving inappropriate expressions of love—intrusion, imposition, rejection, neglect, etc.; finding within the reality of a given relationship ample room to love well.

Plant: An emblem of spring, Primrose grows on banks and in woodland, often in colonies. The 'prima rosa' or first 'rose' of the year.

HEALING QUALITIES

Primrose essence helps us to love with all the boundlessness of our being whilst respecting any boundaries that may exist in the external space of relating. It helps to safe-guard us from drawing inappropriate expressions of love from other people - from neglect through to intrusiveness, lack of care through to excessive intimacy - by enabling us to be more fully conscious of our own boundaries and the level of our needs. Similarly, it helps us to be aware of and accept the needs and boundaries of the other person, comprehending their wishes and desires when they are at odds with our own, coming to an inner acceptance of the place of balance between us.

As such this is a remedy which can be useful in relations with friends and loved ones, helping to heal conflict that may come from misunderstandings about the love that is being offered. The time, heart-space, energy, commitment, etc., available on each side does not always balance; this can cause great confusion, unhappiness, and/or feelings of being compromised. Because the essence facilitates the acceptance of letting love Be at the level it truly is, it can release the struggle and pain around this, bringing greater peace and acceptance.

Primrose helps to cleanse the path of love and make it clear. It holds a very finely balanced energy which helps to tune the frequency of relating between people, to clarify the channel so that all hearts involved are able to communicate clearly and simply and be with the relationship at the level that is comfortable for them. It will enable people to step in or step back, as appropriate, to give the relationship a harmonious space in which to thrive at the level which is a true representation for all concerned.

Indications: *Relationships with others which feel invasive, inappropriate, cruel; where two people are not able to 'meet in the middle'; poor communication in relationships; neediness, dependency, neglect; inability to establish loving boundaries.*

Energetic: Solar Plexus and Heart chakras; Astral body; Celestial body.

I open fully to the love that is here for me

RING OF BRODGAR – *Environmental essence*
KEYNOTE: Sacred Ceremony

Focus; charge point of spiritual intent; cohesion. Helps us to be still within and become aware of the support of the earth and humanity; feeling these coming together in wild and sacred energy; for ceremonies, for recharging, for deep connection with the sacred in earth and sky. Protection for one's own sacred space.

Subject: This Orkney stone circle stands on a strip of land in a loch, surrounded by a low circle of hills and eventually by the sea. The essence was made at dawn in late summer.

HEALING QUALITIES

This environmental essence of the Ring of Brodgar brings focus: to charge and protect one's energy, grounding and connecting one with the forces of Nature and Spirit. It reflects our deep-rooted sense of the sacredness of Life and the wish to celebrate this with ceremony. Inviting us to step in to the strange, mystical and wondrous interaction that exists between Nature, Spirit and Humanity, we enter a profound communion with Life.

Stone circles are places of power, energy, celebration, community and containment. They are an age-old testimony to the need to connect deeply with the forces around us - massive standing stones of hewn rock placed in the teeth of the elements, in a perfect circle, aligned with the stars. Circles within circles, they evoke the wheel of life, mandalas, chakra wheels, that which never ends or begins; a container for energy, both keeping in and keeping out. The Ring of Brodgar, far to the north of Britain, on a strip of land almost surrounded by water, is a most beautiful example of this: at once elemental, pagan and wild, and yet deeply peaceful and protective.

Ring of Brodgar facilitates going through rites of passage, or in periods that must be marked with ceremony and awareness. It helps contain and charge the energy within and around, enabling us to connect with the depth, solemnity, and celebration of such times. It assists in creating and holding a sacred space, imbuing it with the mystical energy, peace and gentleness of this far northern stone circle. Finally, it is an essence to recharge, bring cohesion to, ground and protect one's energy at any time where this is needed.

Indications: *Scattered, unfocused energy; lack of sacred ceremony and intent around the important things in one's life; lack of awareness of the resource of the earth's energy and wisdom; feeling energetically vulnerable and unprotected.*

Energetic: Root, Sacral, Brow and Crown chakras.

I celebrate the sacredness of Life

RUBY-IN-THE-STORM – *Gem/Environmental Essence*
KEYNOTE: *Strength of Heart*

Staying firmly grounded in one's heart during times of cataclysmic change; going with the dynamic winds of change, even when these seem shattering; releasing one's self to movement whilst staying absolutely centred in the heart; charting the path of heart through the storm.

Subject: My husband brought this gem of raw ruby in zoisite to me as a gift on the day I was to graduate from my Energy Healing training. Moments after it arrived in the house a storm began outside. Intuitively we placed the gem in a bowl in the garden to make an essence of this energy. Leaving the valley to go to my graduation we found calm skies, yet three hours later when we returned, the storm in the valley still raged. The water in the bowl was alive to the hammering of the rain; the gem remained undisturbed. Soon after, the storm passed away, and a new essence was complete.

HEALING QUALITIES

This is an essence which facilitates real strength and grounding during times of change. Ruby-in-the-Storm helps to stabilise the heart-energy amidst profound turmoil, keeping one centred in this loving space. Then everything else may shift and the winds of change may whistle through the heart and through all that one is, but the heart remains steady. It is like having within a sturdy, sea-worthy vessel with which to ride out a turbulent storm.

Ruby-in-the-Storm is for times when we are experiencing the most profound changes in our life where nothing seems familiar to us anymore. It is as if we are standing in our own world but feel incomprehensibly alien within it. Nothing that we knew now feels certain, and there is nothing external that we can grasp hold of.

This essence helps us hold to an inner strength—the stillness at the centre of all motion, of all life, the eye of calm in the middle of the storm. It enables us not to react, not to be blown at will by every gust that comes our way. Instead we respond firmly and clearly, finding our way through, holding to that which we do know and which supports and sustains us. In this way, we can let go of beliefs or ways of being which no longer serve us or which hold us back.

Indications: *Feeling as if one's heart is too frail to bear the circumstances you are in; feeling caught in a storm – externally or internally; being without an inner anchor; feeling out of control of events; the heart under pressure or stress; intense emotional turmoil.*

Energetic: Root, Heart and Crown chakras.

My heart is strong and steady

SCOTS PINE SENTINEL – *Pinus sylvestris*
KEYNOTE: Inner Direction

Helps us to re-orientate when feeling lost, blind, seemingly stuck in the past;
for being with the fog and seeing through it; maintaining smooth strong
boundaries to aura; brings warmth, security and sense of being at home.

Plant: This grove of Scots Pines is found on the shores of Loch Garten in the Cairngorms. Here the trees grow straight and true. The essence was made one quiet silvery dawn, with the bowl placed in the exposed roots of the tree.

HEALING QUALITIES

Scots Pine Sentinel assists us in discerning, heeding and staying connected with our internal compass. In times when we feel lost and afraid it supports us in finding our bearings, coming back to the space within where we know where we are and where we need to go, no matter how disorientating it may be for us in the external world. It reminds us that we have everything we could possibly need now to deal with this moment and that nothing that we have been given to deal with is beyond our capabilities. The essence supports us when we feel lost and stuck, when we are faced by a wall of fog which we cannot see through, where the path ahead is no longer clear. This can make one feel anxious, unsure of what to do and liable to act from a place of panic rather than from an internal space of calm and confidence.

Scots Pine Sentinel nurtures feelings of deep grounding and certainty. It encourages the ability to wait patiently in unfamiliar times to see how things unfold - not reacting but trusting the deeper plan that we often cannot see or fathom. In this place of trust we are always at home, always safe, always at the centre where we need to be, always open to the support that surrounds us on all levels. Here our energy-field can remain strong and intact, our aura not weakened by fears and doubts, our stamina consistent. The essence assists us in staying connected with this space with a smooth strong aura.

Indications: *Lost and afraid; disconnected from internal compass and sense of where and why; impatient, frustrated, confused; in limbo and out of balance; unsettled and not able to 'feel at home' in oneself or one's world; ungrounded; feeling ill-equipped to deal with the times you are in.*

Energetic: Root and Crown chakras; Ketheric Template.

I follow my inner direction

SCOTS PRIMROSE – *Primula scotica*
KEYNOTE: Jewel of the Heart

The 'Heart Support' essence; restores exquisite connection with the heart, with its deepest potential; nurtures a deep jewel-like resonance of energy in the heart - with life, with one's self and with others; enables you intimately to explore the heart's deeper treasures.

Plant: Scots Primrose is an incredibly rare and diminutive plant, found in only a handful of locations in northern Scotland and the Orkneys. Here, landowners carefully protect its habitat, giving this tiny plant every possible opportunity to flourish.

HEALING QUALITIES

The exquisite flower-head of the Scots Primrose consists of tiny heart-shaped petals of rich magenta, clustered around a golden centre. It is the 'heart support' essence: it helps us reach for the deepest treasures of our heart and deeply connect with qualities of love, compassion and forgiveness. It assists us in engaging more intimately with ourselves and others, connecting heart-to-heart, openly and with joy.

The essence evokes the beauty of the heart's energy and of its phenomenal capacities for love. It is a place of great depth, richness, and treasures – a constantly present resource that connects us with our most enduring and humane qualities. Intimacy, the ability to forgive another, acceptance, unconditional love, passion and romance, tenderness, compassion, integrity, faithfulness, and 'determination to live and respond as a peaceful being' – these are all gifts the heart offers, seeds of potential within us all. Scots Primrose helps find and anchor these qualities within ourselves. It reminds us of the radiance of our heart's energy, its jewel-like glow and warmth, its depth and beauty. And it invites us to put this radiance at the centre of our being and of our life.

This is an essence which is particularly suited to taking long-term as it gently transmutes, opens and brings light to more and more of your heart, gradually revealing the beauty therein.

Indications: *Going to deeper depths with the heart; breaking through old patterns that restrict one's ability to love; an experience which deeply affects the heart and calls for a new level of response.*

Energetic: Heart chakra; Astral body; Celestial body.

I enjoy deep love and intimacy

SELF HEAL – *Prunella vulgaris*
KEYNOTE: Self-nurture

Awareness of your healing needs; self-nurture and self-care; understanding the language of the body and its symptoms. Trusting the body's healing wisdom. Turning from a path of self-destruction back towards healing; letting go of habits which lead to ill-health.

Plant: This essence was made in the Cumbrian fells when the plant was throwing out its last flowers after a long season and already held the seed-heads for its future propagation.

HEALING QUALITIES

Self Heal is an essence which helps us to understand the call of our body to heal. It helps us to soften and surrender to the level our body actually is at rather than at the level we think it should be. It assists us in recognising our healing needs, changing any potentially damaging trajectory we may be on in life and correcting this for one that is more nurturing. Our well-being is intimately linked with our ability to read and understand the communications of our body through our thoughts, feelings and physical symptoms. The more we are sensible of and connected with this inner feedback, the more we are able to live happy and fulfilling lives.

Self Heal helps us to fall in love with the vital process of self-care. This is not as a hypochondriacal obsession with our bodily symptoms but a mindful inner process where we respect the message of our body when it is telling us we are out of balance, and heed its call to return to a more harmonious way of being. This self-knowledge is truly a prerequisite for healing. Learning to flow with our health rather than against it makes life sweeter and more enjoyable.

In knowing oneself we are each better able to understand and bring support to the healing needs of others. The other common name for this plant is 'All Heal'. Healing oneself inevitably leads to the healing of others. And at a deeper level, by our very vibration of wholeness, we subliminally touch the fabric of all life with our mindfulness and vitality; our presence becomes a balm.

Indications: *Inability to love, nurture and care for the self; ignoring warning signs in body; pushing beyond one's limits; lack of self-care, self-knowledge, bodily connection; unhealthy patterns and habits; unwillingness to take the steps to healing.*

Energetic: Solar Plexus, Heart, Throat, Brow and Crown chakras. Etheric body, Astral level, Etheric Template, Causal level.

I lovingly care for myself

Alight Within

SERENITY – *Environmental Essence*
KEYNOTE: *Mindfulness*

Provides an inner bridge for stepping from one level of awareness / consciousness to the next; for releasing attachment to any clouds passing over the clear blue sky of the eternal mind; grace, mindfulness, awareness.

Subject: This essence was made on the shores of Mull as the sun set behind Iona, casting its rays upon this holy island and across the tranquil water.

HEALING QUALITIES

Serenity is an essence which nurtures an internal space for meditation, mindfulness and increased awareness. It assists us in moving from one level of consciousness to another, releasing resistance and moving gently and fluidly forward to greater openness and clarity. It is a profoundly supportive tool for spiritual practice, helping us to let go of Need and enjoy the serenity of Being.

The essence is also helpful where there is suffering and turmoil that comes from undue attachment to a way of being/a person/a set of circumstances/ an ideal or dream. The deep soothing calm of the environment in which this essence was made - the sea hushed and at peace - acts like a spiritual balm. Serenity assists us in bringing awareness and wisdom to those processes of the mind which can judge, undermine, and sabotage us, causing us to distort what is beautiful, simple and natural within ourselves. It helps gently to untangle the knots and release us from patterns of clinging desperately to that which is external to us.

The essence invites us to rest in the knowledge that we reside in a world of grace and miracles; to trust to its unfolding, aware and open, discerning our way through.

Indications: *Difficulty coping with changes which require new ways of seeing, responding, understanding; mental chatter; difficulty in meditating; mental confusion and disarray; lack of clarity, peace and awareness; clouded mind.*

Energetic: Throat, Brow and Crown chakras; Ketheric Template.

*I awaken to new levels of
consciousness*

SILVER BIRCH 'FIRE'– *Betula pendula*
KEYNOTE: Harnessing Fire

For learning to master one's fire, letting it flow without burn-out or overwhelm; walking in the realms of anger and passion without going into reaction; helps us feel our way through to gifts of insight, inner power and self-awareness.

Subject: This essence was made by placing a bowl in the roots of Silver Birch trees in the old forests of the Cairngorms, Scotland. The tree selected had deep red-brown skins under the peeling bark and looked as if it were on fire.

HEALING QUALITIES

Silver Birch 'Fire' essence facilitates a strong and grounded wielding of one's own fire. It is for staying anchored in one's power and not being overwhelmed by the emotions of passion and anger or the ego's wish to control. It is like being within a 'fire wall' of protection which enables one to stay detached but compassionate when meeting these emotions in self and others. As we remain contained in the face of our fiery nature and do not react from it, we begin to harness its energy in more positive ways—to strengthen our commitment, resolution, vision, scope, determination. It fosters warrior energy—teaching us of the potential to harness passion for peace.

This essence helps with the visionary aspects of the fire element—for being wise enough and quick enough to see. It works to burn away illusion, enabling a person to see more clearly (even piercingly) into areas of one's life and being, where this may be needed.

Silver Birch helps with true mastery of one's most potent emotions—for being able to contact them, draw on them, use their vision and potency, but not be consumed by their power. It cools and grounds reaction, teaching one to sit within the furnace of one's passion and wield its energy discerningly - with patience, peacefully - and thus learn the gentle nature of true Power.

Indications: *Being at the mercy of one's anger/passion/fiery nature; feeling out of control and unable to judge correctly and act with awareness; destructive patterns of anger which are harming precious areas of one's life; seeing 'red'; energy expended explosively, not effectively; caught in conflict and struggling to restore peace.*

Energetic: Root, Solar Plexus and Brow chakras; Emotional body.

I harness my passion for peace

SILVER LIGHT– *Environmental essence*
KEYNOTE: *Patient Stillness*

For stillness, for attending/awaiting change; for those times when it is not right for us to act, for learning the gift of patient attention; understanding the energy of winter when nothing appears to be happening; staying poised and gathering for the moment when action is needed.

Subject: This essence was made on a day when the first breath of spring broke through the dark months of winter. The ancient oak woodland, in which the essence was made, was utterly still as if time had been suspended. The light was silvery, the air hushed and expectant, and there was a sense of being outside of Time.

HEALING QUALITIES

Silver Light enables us to be with the energy of winter in our lives - metaphorically and literally. It supports us in understanding the worth of times of rest, hibernation and apparent inactivity. Such times may have been forced on us by illness, the failure of a project to get off the ground, lack of employment, etc. It is a time when the ground on which we stand seems cold and hard; nothing appears to be growing. It helps us to be with times of rest and inactivity in our lives, with great patience and trust, poised and ready to act when the moment comes, gathering our resources and strength in this time of grace.

Often we find it difficult to let go into these inactive periods, feeling weighed down by self-judgment that tells us we are failures, unworthy and unable. This essence gently illuminates these patterns of self-criticism, letting us see them for what they are; and it reminds us of the gift that awaits us in being present to the moment.

It is not a time to push but a time to yield and surrender, knowing that snowdrops, daffodils and a new season are incubating beneath.

Indications: *Impatience during times of limbo and uncertainty; feeling that nothing is moving/changing/happening; distrust in the divine order of things; feeling cut off from miracles and grace; unable to change what is; seeking to move beyond the present before accepting it.*

Energetic: Crown chakra; Ketheric Template.

In stillness I am poised and ready

SPRING GREENS - *Environmental Essence*
KEYNOTE: *Healing Environment*

Creating a healing environment; establishing external and internal support and readiness for healing process; a feeling of a strong web of energy which holds one in wholeness; renewal, replenishment and vitality.

Subject: This environmental essence was made in a well-established wood of sessile oak and other deciduous trees at dawn one spring morning, as the light filtered through the green canopy above.

HEALING QUALITIES

Spring Greens essence helps create a supportive internal and external environment for healing. Bursting with the energy of renewal, and the tranquillity of a spring wood, this essence supports our energy matrix in weaving a protective cocoon within which we can safely undertake our healing process.

Imagine walking in a wood on a bright spring day, where the sun streams through the delicate young leaves of oak, ash, birch and beech, creating a wondrous sanctuary filled with soft green light. It is like being in Nature's own cathedral with the high arching boughs of the trees and the hushed tranquillity of the atmosphere. Bluebells, Greater Stitchwort and newly-opening ferns dapple the floor with their colour. It is a place to sit and rest and feel the brimming vitality of Nature seeping into one's core.

This essence helps us to establish, at an energetic level, our inner connections with all aspects of ourselves so that we can bring wholeness to our healing. It is like a web being woven within so that we do not focus on healing a part of ourselves in isolation, but heal as the potent entity we are, in our entirety. This internal environment of support and readiness begins to be reflected outwardly as we find ourselves almost inevitably extending outwards to create an ambience that is conducive to our healing process. This is a wonderful essence to spray in hospital rooms, a sick room, one's house, one's bedroom, whenever you wish to create a wholesome and healing atmosphere. Taken internally it helps us to create the energetic web on which our health can be more strongly woven and preserved.

Indications: *Discordant environment in which to heal; surroundings which do not support one's healing process; lack of readiness internally for the healing process; lack of support at any level for healing; feeling fragmented and not whole when trying to heal; feeling jaded by healing process.*

Energetic: Sacral, Throat and Crown chakras. Etheric Body, Etheric Template and Causal level.

I am held in a healing matrix
of Light

SPRING SQUILL - *Scilla verna*
KEYNOTE: Childhood Innocence

For clarifying and restoring childhood innocence and truth; protects the dreams and innocence of childhood; brings insight and support to trauma, bad dreams, painful experiences, in adults and children; encourages us to stay aligned with and embody the spirit of our childhood dreams.

Subject: This diminutive plant has baby-blue flowers which appear, like stars strewn across a magic carpet, on the turf of grassy headlands in spring.

HEALING QUALITIES

Spring Squill is an essence that preserves, restores and nurtures the innocence and joy of childhood. It can be used equally well for children and adults. The flowers of this plant have a wonderful child-like feel to them. As an essence, Spring Squill helps one to catch one's star, keeping one's dreams and sense of destiny clear and intact. Our life-dreams begin in childhood. It is incredibly important that these are nurtured, encouraged and developed at an early age – thereby giving us our own inner magic carpet as a foundation from which to fly as we go through life. The essence can be used at key stages in a child's life when they, or their guardians, face difficult and life-changing decisions. This essence will help them remain connected with the star that guides them and the joy they have within. As adults it helps us to recover our early dreams, with the innocence and delight that permeates them.

At a deeper level, Spring Squill helps to turn back trauma in childhood. Where a child has been abused or experienced deep pain, where life has literally been a 'bad dream', the essence helps deeply to cleanse and restore childhood truth and innocence, energetically wiping the slate clean. Such experiences can often cause a child to seem older than they are and to be more serious, cautious and guarded. They can also lead to difficulty sleeping /night terrors. The essence, along with appropriate action and love, helps restore a child's sense of magic, trust, curiosity, play, and joy. It invites them to come back to the spirit of childhood with the incredible gifts and healing it offers. In a similar way, for adults who have missed out on their childhood for whatever reason, this essence offers healing, solace and magic to the child within. It reminds us of the stars in the night sky, inviting us to wish upon them.

Indications: *Children suffering from nightmares, fears, etc.; coming out of and healing trauma from childhood; inability to connect with child-like joy and innocence; loss of connection with childhood dreams.*

Energetic: Sacral, Throat and Crown chakras.

*I embrace child-like innocence
and joy*

STARRY SAXIFRAGE - *Saxifraga stellaris*
KEYNOTE: Spiritual and Earthly Balance

Supports us in balancing our needs for worldly success, achievement and recognition, with our spiritual values; helps us accept and harness our material desires so they can work in harmony with our spiritual needs to create true wholistic abundance for our self and others.

Subject: Starry Saxifrage has star-like white flowers with a deep red central fruit. It grows in bogs on peaty ground, often high in the mountains.

HEALING QUALITIES

Starry Saxifrage helps us to balance our spiritual path with our material nature - our higher purpose with our desires, ambitions, ego and drive. It helps to marry the energy of the two productively in truly holistic success and abundance. It is an essence that fosters a powerful integrity between these two differing aspects of one's being - the white petals of spirit embracing and holding in safety the yellow and red of the fire and dynamism within. Ego is not something we can do away with - it is a fundamental part of who we are, a touchstone to return to and check in with. However, when out of awareness it can become out of balance, driving us to become caught up in the world of externals, competing for recognition and attention as if this were all that matters.

Starry Saxifrage helps to balance ego by keeping us in contact with our spirituality and enabling this more tangibly to permeate our material life. It invites us to give up aggressiveness, competition, and self-indulgence where these put us at odds with self and others. Instead it supports us in harnessing drive and ambition as forces of potent creativity, at the disposal of Spirit.

Indications: *Overly concerned with material and worldly success; lack of connection with deeper spiritual values of one's work and creativity; fearful of releasing one's work to Spirit as a source for good; caught up in the external world of material needs and forgetting to connect with the deeper reality of Spirit or unable to turn spiritual insights into worldly success and abundance; imbalance between work and material reward.*

Energetic: Root, Sacral and Crown chakras.

*I balance my spiritual and
worldly needs*

VENUS TRANSIT– *Flower/Astrological Essence*
KEYNOTE: Divine Feminine

Opening to the energy of the Divine Female; exploring and knowing the energies of goddess, fertility, intuition, birth, destruction within; initiation into the inner magic and mystery of the Feminine.

Subject: This essence was made during the transit of Venus across the sun on 8th June 2004. The astrological essence also contained the flower of a wild rose which only flowered on this one occasion.

HEALING QUALITIES

Venus Transit assists with unifying the male and female energies within us, with particular emphasis on bringing the feminine energy fully into power where this has been over-ridden by the energy of maleness.

It is an essence that speaks of the sacredness of the heart and of love, and of the power of these to bring beauty, grace and healing to our lives. It invites us to commune anew with the heart of life in a way which acknowledges fully its sacred nature and our own. It teaches us to listen more deeply - beyond the physical, material, rational, doctrinal - to that which is pervasive, encompassing, embracing, and mystical, within all life. The energy of goddess, mother earth, the Divine Feminine. This is an energy which has, throughout the world, symbolised the forces of life and death, of destruction and rebirth, of instinct and intuition, of deep knowing of the pattern of things, and of the reading of these patterns.

For women this essence deeply connects one to this feminine power, returning to the fore the powers of mothering, destroying, birthing, bringing forth, intuiting, knowing, sexuality, sensuality, and the weaving of love. It helps a woman to reconnect with her feminine ancestry and heritage.

For men it particularly helps to be open to the sensual and sensitive aspects of the Venus energy within themselves and from others.

It restores balance and brings healing where this energy has been misrepresented or stifled in a person's life, helping them to connect to it safely and with wonderment, feeling the power of it to heal.

Indications: *Unable to connect with one's feminine nature; divorced from the feminine; sterile female energies – inability to nurture self and others, create and destroy, surrender, release, move on, embrace, accept; overly Yang energies in women or men; lack of connection with the Divine Feminine.*

Energetic: Sacral, Heart and Crown chakras; Yin qualities in harmony and balance with Yang.

I open to the Divine Feminine

VERNAL EQUINOX - *Environmental Essence*
KEYNOTE: *Sacral Balance*

Awakening sexual energy; regeneration of the sacral chakra. Cleansing and clearing the sacral chakra of obstruction

Subject: This gem essence was made at the Spring Equinox 2009, on a brilliantly clear day as the sun arose. Snow still lay on the mountains and the sky above was blue. The air felt clean and vibrant. The essence is made by suspending the gem in a bowl inside a bowl of spring water.

HEALING QUALITIES

Vernal Equinox essence supports the awakening of dormant sexual energies and the regeneration of the sacral chakra. It is an essence which helps to re-establish flow; energetic cleanliness; and life, creativity and expression being ready to come forth. Vernal Equinox helps gently to ease out energetic blocks to this. It calls forth new life and energy in this area, and brings strength, renewal and support.

The essence is useful where there has been a shutting down of the sacral or where it has never fully opened. It encourages the energy to flow in this area and to flower. It is safe, supportive, and suitable for use even where there is a lot of fear of one's sacral power. The sacral chakra is where our sexuality, our procreativity, our creativity, and physical intimacy spring from. And it is the seat of incredibly vital energy which needs to be flowing in order for us to experience full health. Vernal Equinox is of use wherever there are recurrent problems in the sacral area and where there is resistance to sexual expression and blossoming.

Indications: *Sexual energy out of balance – too much or too little; inability to access sexual energy in a loving and healthy way; poor vitality; possible issues with abundance, wealth, mothering, creativity.*

Energetic: Root, Sacral and Throat chakra; Etheric body.

*I embrace and flow with my
sexual energy*

VIPER'S BUGLOSS - *Echium vulgare*
KEYNOTE: *Sacred Discourse*

Knowing the true weight of words and their potential for harm or healing; releasing the need to criticise, judge, blame, condemn; coming to a place of care and creativity with one's language; learning own sacred discourse.

Subject: This tall stately plant has incredibly deep roots – once it has taken hold, it is difficult to uproot. Its long hairy stalks are punctuated with the funnel-shaped flowers which are pink in the bud and become blue once in full flower. This bi-coloured effect of the flowers is part of its beauty and these somewhat tender colours contrast sharply with its rough stem.

HEALING QUALITIES

This essence reflects the fact that the power of speech is one of our greatest gifts. It is the power to articulate, to inspire others, to move beyond separateness to communion, to soothe, to amuse, to inform, to tell stories, to love, to wax lyrical.

Viper's Bugloss reawakens an awareness of the words we use, their full weight and impact. It helps us with the spoken word, particularly where the joy and awareness of communication is at a low level and speech has become negative or critical. Words can be 'swords' which can harshly pierce the defences of another, deceive people, and indeed control and manipulate them. This includes the words that are our internal thoughts which may also damage and control us, negating the beauty of who we are. Viper's Bugloss invites us to seek for a better way to use words, a way which is more insightful and aware, a way which understands their ripple-effect, a way which is more aligned with our higher intent.

Words are a fundamental tool in creating the world we live in—our own immediate environment. They profoundly reflect who we are, what we put out, what our intentions and motivations are, how we relate to others. This essence helps to temper those areas of speech where we are not aware and where the message we put across is not what we truly wish to create. It releases the sharpness, the barbs of inappropriate speech, enabling us to find a gentler, softer way; a way which does not shut others out and which releases us to be much more articulate about who we really are.

Indications: *Overly critical of self and others; language is damaging – violent, hard, judgmental, or negating; controlling others through one's discourse; struggling to use words wisely and well; putting one's self or others down; seeking a more loving discourse.*

Energetic: Throat, Heart and Crown chakras.

My words are my sacred discourse

NEW ESSENCES

FROG ORCHID *(Coeloglossum viride)*
Miracles

Miracles happen and prayers are answered. Joyfully opening to this without expectation or demand; letting go of how or what comes; connecting with the deep and magical wishes of the heart; opening to the flow of Universal response, aligning with this and trusting deeply to its unfolding; releasing the need to grasp or determine outcomes; enjoying the co-creative process of dancing with Life.

MOONWORT *(Botrychium lunaria)*
Language of the unconscious

Understanding how Life, our bodies, our unconscious all communicate with us; symbolism, dreams, imagery, symptoms; deeper meaning and significance; becoming more aware of and aligned with rich inner sources of illumination and guidance; accessing the dream state when awake, to see life shamanically.

ONE-FLOWERED WINTERGREEN *(Moneses uniflora)*
Good in all things

Being able to see that we are part of a Benevolent Universe; opening to and deeply accepting the good in all things; moving beyond narrow-mindedness, prejudice and judgment to an acceptance and trust of What Is; willingness to receive the goodness and benevolence of the Universe fully and spread this to others through one's thoughts, words and actions.

TWINFLOWER *(Linnaea borealis)*
Sensing needs

Harmony of understanding in close or one-to-one relationships; heartfelt communication; sensing the way of flow between each other; correct interpretation; reading accurately and sensitively 'between the lines' through subtle signs, intuition, deep listening; balancing of Yin and Yang in close communication and relations.

COMBINATION ESSENCES

These are special combinations of single essences for generic situations which we can reach for with confidence when we need to. They are very good in the acute – for example we can use **Light Support** in situations where we feel shock, trauma, darkness or distress; and where we feel lacking in confidence and inner strength and need quickly to regain our connection with our centre. However they can also be used when we are faced with longer term difficulties. In such situations we can take an essence combination as a deep-acting constitutional support to help us shift out of a particular theme or situation that is predominant in our life.

The combinations have each taken several years to make – usually four years from start to finish – which is much longer than the gestation, manifestation and testing period of the majority of the single essences. This is because the combinations are a deep marrying of specific single essences, each with their own unique character. In combining them the aim is that they ultimately sing together - resonant and harmonious - able fully to realise the gift of the theme they touch. So **Heart Balm** not only tends and soothes the heart's wounds; it helps us to go more deeply into the riches of our heart and live from a more loving place within it, radiating this out to others. **Bountiful Life** not only helps us move towards greater abundance in our life; it also increases our awareness of our ability to give, receive and have gratitude; to know our heart's desire and move towards it; and to understand that abundance is not just about our material needs but is something we can dance with on every level of our being.

The process of combining the essences is one of listening – listening to the theme and how this is out of joint in the world, how people struggle with it and what qualities would help them to be able to move through it more easily, naturally and gently; listening to the essences to see which answer the call and which can hold strong a part of the energy for us so that we can find our footing once more; listening to how each works with the other and if they can be life-long partners in this combination, this song; and listening to the responses within myself and others when the essence is tested and used.

Once the essences are selected, the mother tinctures are combined together in water and blessed to create a new mother tincture for this combination. It is then made up using the normal process so that the combination essence is consolidated and refined by the time it reaches the stock essence level. The combination is now one essence - individual voices in synergy providing a broad but delicate brush-stroke to support our insight and healing - an essence that is more than the sum of its parts. Here we have something that we can trust to hold us well, support our unfolding, but also galvanise us when things are difficult. The combinations bring a sense of weaving a web of support, a matrix of energy scintillating and light-filled, which will help us move beyond this particular pattern.

How do we use these in contrast to single essences? The combination essences can be reached for at any time we need to work with their particular theme:

Bountiful Life - creating an abundant life which richly answers our heart's desires.

Healer's Light - connecting deeply with our capacity to heal and the inner path of this healing, for ourselves and others.

Heart Balm - enabling the heart to blossom in loving tenderness, healing the wounds of the past.

Light Support - being centred in our inner light and strength when we are going through personal challenges and dark times.

Loving Desire - for love, intimacy, sensuality and sexuality and a healthy, fulfilling connection with these in ourselves and another.

Animal Support - to create a loving, secure atmosphere for our animal friends, helping them assimilate change and upheaval.

BOUNTIFUL LIFE COMBINATION

To help you attract benevolent abundance into your life; assists you in manifesting abundance in line with your deeper self.

Bountiful Life Combination brings together flower, gem and environmental essences which facilitate us being in the flow of abundance. It helps us move beyond the quick-fix solutions of many modern-day approaches to abundance which focus only on material gain and often leave us feeling dissatisfied, driven solely by our wants. Bountiful Life helps us feel for our personal values in life - those qualities we wish to embody and to have more fully present, those experiences and resources which are truly of worth to us - and thus create a life of harmony and fulfilment which spans all levels.

Golden Light – This essence supports us in creating the life of our dreams. It is an essence of optimism and playfulness. It serves to clear our mind and emotions of negativity and despondency relating to our beliefs about creating the life we truly wish to live. With this essence we can look forward to manifesting a future which is bright, sacred and blessed.

Hawthorn Berries – In order to create a fulfilling life we must be able to connect with and work towards our heart's desire. The Hawthorn's berries hold the accumulation of the previous year's growth cycle and store the seeds for the coming year. The essence helps us to receive the fruits of our labour so that we do not continue to work incessantly and forget to enjoy the beauty we have created so far.

Hawthorn Blossom – When creating benevolent abundance in our lives it is important that we have gratitude for what we already have. Our future happiness rests on our understanding and welcoming the gifts that are currently in our life; from these we will weave what is yet to come. This essence helps us bless our current abundance and gratefully move this forward.

Marsh Felwort – Our inner wisdom constantly speaks to us of ways in which we can more skilfully, and with greater sophistication, navigate our way through daily life. Heeding and applying this wisdom, we are able to bring our spiritual clarity to a more pragmatic and practical use. Marsh Felwort strengthens our insight and our discipline in applying this so that we are more productive in what we achieve.

Marsh Marigold – Open-mindedness and clarity of mind help us attract appropriate abundance and utilise it. When the mind is overworked through excessive planning, problem-solving and left-brain activity we become fatigued, lacking the spontaneity to respond more creatively to life. Marsh Marigold helps to support the easy optimism and clarity of a mind that is free to work both rationally and intuitively.

Scots Pine Sentinel – This essence helps us to feel grounded and certain, sure of our path forward. When we are moving into new territory, broaching new horizons, expanding our comfort zone, we need to be sure that we can navigate from an internal compass that guides us on our way with our values intact. Scots Pine Sentinel keeps us certain and at home within, so that we do not lose our head.

Vernal Equinox – The sacral chakra is the part of our energy-body and being that relates to creativity, procreation and money. Ensuring that the energy is flowing here enables us to slip more easily into the currents of abundance and find our way in these waters with greater skill. Vernal Equinox gently supports us in this process, releasing blocks to flow in the sacral chakra.

This combination helps us to move beyond limiting beliefs around abundance. It supports us in knowing that we are worthy of and capable of creating the life of our dreams, and receiving our heart's desires. It is a combination which teaches us the cycle of abundance – the importance of being able to give, receive and at all times have gratitude for what has been, what is and what is yet to be, so that we may continue to keep the wheel turning. With the help of this combination we learn to trust that we have everything we need to create the life we wish for. In this moment is the seed for all that is to come. It also brings us to the deeper insight that personal abundance is a spiritual matter and that it touches us all. We cannot create a truly beautiful life without touching others around us in similar ways.

The combination affects us on many levels, but in particular it can be used as follows:

To **align energetically** with the abundance that is around you at all times.

To **open to receiving appropriate manifestations of abundance** which concur with your spiritual path.

To connect with your **heart's desires** and the **life of your dreams**.

To learn to **discern, magnetise and move towards** healthy and fulfilling abundance.

To **see abundance where before you have only seen lack**.

To **release negative patterns of blocking** joyous and bounteous abundance.

At deeper levels, and over a longer period of time, we can use Bountiful Life to create ever more mindfully and beautifully the life of our desires, in line with our spiritual truth. In doing this we can then touch others and support them in stepping into greater abundance and flow; and the fruits of our labours can be shared and enjoyed with others.

Bountiful Life Mist can be sprayed around your aura to help draw to you abundant and joyful experiences and people that support you in manifesting a beautiful life. It can be used in your work place to help you stay connected with your joy and your play in the midst of your work. At times when someone is embarking on a new project or a new period of creativity, it is incredibly supportive of this process. It reminds us of the true nature of abundance as that which stems from our heart and makes ourselves and all around us feel good.

Bountiful Life Mist contains:
Bountiful Life Combination and organic essential oils of Ylang Ylang, Black Spruce, Frankincense, Orange, Myrtle and Cinnamon.

HEALER'S LIGHT COMBINATION

To support your healing process; to connect you with your vital force and your subtle energy matrix; to assist you in assimilating higher levels of health and wellbeing.

Healer's Light Combination brings together flower and environmental essences which together support you on your healing journey, helping you to connect with the vitality at your core and move in harmony with this to establish deeper levels of wellbeing. It assists you in listening more deeply to your energy, becoming familiar with the feeling of health within you and the patterns of dis-ease that take you away from this. It is an essence to support your healing wisdom and your ability to heed and work with this.

Bogbean – Bogbean helps us to attune to our own and another person's needs with accuracy and awareness. It is an essence which serves to refine our ability to sense, and to bring balance and discernment to this. Many who are in the healing profession find it difficult to protect themselves from other peoples' energy – they often feel like a 'sponge', picking up on and becoming overloaded by the thoughts, emotions and energy of others. This essence helps establish a healthy, balanced and stable ability to tune to energy, and to discern when and where this is appropriate. It helps with a practitioner's boundaries and, for ourselves in our own healing, it helps us to sense more clearly the way forward.

Butterfly Orchid – This angelic flower assists us in channelling spiritual energy for healing. When we are healing ourselves or others it is easy to think that we only have our own energy and resources to draw on. This essence enables us more actively to bring in a constant stream of energy from Source which refreshes our energy-body and makes us cleaner and lighter conduits for healing. It also helps those undergoing healing treatments to receive only a clean and pure source of energy from the practitioner and their tools.

Herb Paris – The highly structured nature of this incredible plant gives some indication of its use as an essence which supports our physical and energetic structures and systems. This essence touches us at the pre-physical level where we concomitantly exist and function in a state which is pristine and free from illness. Herb Paris connects us back to this very strongly, enabling us to pull this blueprint through into our energetic matrix to increase our levels of healing and vitality.

Lady's Slipper Orchid – As a plant, Lady's Slipper Orchid feels potent and alive. It helps us to reconnect with our inner healing potency, our life-force, our vitalism. When we are working with the healing of others or our own healing, we come upon times when we feel despair at the task of healing ahead of us and we can feel that healing is not possible. This essence reminds us that healing *is* and there is no other alternative! It enables us to reconnect with what this means for this individual now and to let go of any preconceptions which may stand in the way of our true progress, on whatever level of our being that most directly touches.

Self Heal – This is the essence of self-nurture. The essence helps us to connect with our healing needs, to accept the level of healing we currently have and to continue to move forward in our process. Self Heal teaches us how to nourish ourselves on all levels and helps us to fall in love with this vital process. Learning mindfully to scan one's energy, heed the information we receive and act accordingly to support and uphold ourselves keeps us fresh, strong and able to live life sweetly and happily. In turn we touch others with this and our vitality ripples out in miraculous ways.

Spring Greens – This environmental essence supports us in creating the energetic ambience which enables healing to take place. It brings us the light and energy of earth's renewal and replenishment in spring time, helping us connect with this within ourselves; and Spring Greens helps us to manifest the internal and external environment that is truly propitious for healing. We are reminded that new life is possible, that the body endlessly renews itself and that we are re-creating today what we will live and be tomorrow. It is a calming essence that brings energies of tranquillity and hope.

The essences in this combination together bring us to a greater cognition of what healing is and how this moves within and through us. There is a predominance of green and white flowers here – the colours most conducive to physical healing. The lovely environmental essence, Spring Greens, embodies the tangible feel of this in a deciduous wood in springtime where the soft new verdant leaves filter green light through the canopy and create a feeling of sanctuary, of being in Nature's cathedral. With this combination we are learning about health at the most intimate and pertinent levels for our own journey through life. But in doing so, we are also learning about health in general. The essence, Self Heal, is also known by the name All Heal: by healing ourselves we are then able to assist in the healing of others.

Healer's Light was made both to help us on our personal journey to healing and to assist those who work in the healing professions. In such a profession it is easy to become drained, to give one's own energy away, to be unable to switch off when people need one's help. This combination helps you to maintain a strong contact with your own healing needs, knowing that you can only be effective for others if you are strong and vibrant yourself. And it enables you to channel healing energy from Spirit so that your own reserves are constantly cleansed and replenished. In particular, it can be used as follows:

To **tone, soothe and balance the subtle energy matrix**, the pre-physical blueprint that upholds our being; to enable this pristine structure to be known and felt more tangibly at a physical level.

To help us **connect more deeply with our healing vitality**, our life-force, and the way it wishes to move through us with greatest harmony, and **to come into balance with this.**

To assist us when we **feel despair of recovery** and have forgotten our innate and miraculous ability to heal.

To help us to **understand the true nature of healing** as it pertains to us at this time.

To establish and maintain **patterns and habits which uphold our health and wellbeing**, and which are based on true self-nurture and body wisdom.

To **assimilate greater levels of healing throughout our entire being** so that we are able to keep moving forward on our path and do not become afraid of the new vitality and potency we feel within ourselves.

To enable us to **draw healing energy from the Universal Energy Field**, rather than relying solely on our own resources.

To protect, support and **keep clean and light** the energy of practitioners who are working with the health of others; to keep them connected with Spirit and the wisdom of their inner healer as a sensitive and congruent conduit for healing.

At deeper levels, and over a longer period of time, we can use Healer's Light to help us connect more and more deeply with what Health is in our own body and being, and in that of others. It helps us to attune to the well-being of the systems and organs of our body, understanding more fully how they work together in wholeness, and how we can support that. As we begin to cultivate our 'health-sense', we begin to be aware of how the people, animals and environment around us may move towards better health. We develop an instinctive feel for health and the direction in which it lies.

Healer's Light Mist brings the fresh green smell of herbs, combined with delicate floral notes, to help us to reconnect with the Earth and all its bounty, feeling its wonderful revitalizing health within. It creates an uplifting atmosphere through its fresh and vital scent. You can use the mist to spray around a sick room daily; for your house when you feel under-par / wish to connect more deeply with your Inner Healer / when you wish to energetically protect against sickness; or for your aura when you wish to strengthen your connection with your own vital force and your subtle energy systems.

For healers and therapists, I recommend Healer's Light Mist and Light Support Mist as two essential tools to help maintain a healing space. Light Support clarifies and releases any negative energy, effectively cleaning the therapeutic space between clients and renewing it at the start and end of the day. Healer's Light Mist supports an environment of healing, vitality and insight. It supports the therapist in staying attuned to healing guidance and to the deep potential for healing, and helps the patient remain safe and intact in their energy, and open to new healing insights and real progress.

Healer's Light Mist contains: *Healer's Light Combination and organic essential oils of Palmarosa, Vetiver, Cardamon, Sweet Inula and Chamomile German.*

HEART BALM COMBINATION

To support the gentle beauty and radiance of your heart; to enhance and deepen feelings of love, intimacy and tenderness.

Heart Balm Combination brings together flower and gem essences which together help nurture the radiant and beautiful energy of your heart. It assists you in connecting deeply with and coming from your heart, in tenderness and strength. The combination helps you to stay heart-centred, loving and trusting.

Alpine Willowherb – This essence gently and tenderly acts as a balm for the heart's pain. For wounds we have received in the past through the loss of loved ones, the ending of a relationship, rejection, abandonment, etc., this essence touches them with delicacy and poignancy, enabling us to go to the heart of our pain and release it to healing. Where the heart feels shut down, it helps it to radiate its loving energy once more.

Bluebell – Over time, life can erode our trust in Love and make us feel that it does not exist, that we are not capable of it or that we are unlovable. We begin to distrust our earlier dreams and fantasies and grow suspicious and cynical. Bluebell helps to restore our trust in Love, not as ideals but as a mature yet innocent and delightful journey we undertake with our nearest and dearest.

Grand Quintile – Defensiveness in the heart energy comes from the belief that we are all separate. Grand Quintile supports us in dissolving defences that are outdated and fear-based by inviting us to return to a place where communication is of the Heart and Spirit. It reminds us that we are all One and in this space we are naturally protected for there is no 'other' to attack, only the greater Self to love. From this awareness we are able to extend and receive love with unconditional compassion.

Greater Cuckooflower – At the core of all relationships is the ability to connect with another's heart. Friendship, intimacy, closeness and community all stem from our willingness to engage with another with openness, trust and integrity. This essence helps us to overcome shyness, awkwardness, fears and reluctance when it comes to taking up the opportunity to love and connect with others. It is the essence to help us with nurturing close and enduring friendships and relationships.

Primrose – Not all relationships are based on an ability to meet each other at an equal level with love and accord. Where there is imbalance – where one gives more than another, one needs more space but the other needs more intensity, where one is too intrusive or the other too aloof and removed – this essence helps to return the relationship to its balance point. It guides us to loving appropriately and well, given the needs of both the parties involved, with our heart engaged truthfully.

Scots Primrose – Our heart is like a jewel within us and we may only know some of its riches. This diminutive and rare flower, with its heart-shaped petals, helps us to uncover the deeper qualities of the heart and its phenomenal capacity for human and divine love. It brings us towards greater intimacy, the ability to forgive, acceptance, tenderness, integrity, compassion, etc. It lights the way and shows us the limitless potential within our heart, inviting us deeper and deeper into its treasures.

This combination supports us in sitting within the peaceful radiance of our loving heart. It helps to reveal and enable further exquisite blossoming of this with incredible delicacy and tenderness. Heart Balm supports us in becoming softer and more open in the heart, able to relate to, resonate with and reveal the love in others as we do so. People refer to this as a 'hug in a bottle' because of the way it feels so warm and nurturing to the heart chakra. The three pink flower essences help to tune us to the healthy vibration of this chakra; the gem essences establish the cosmic and physical structure for this; and the final two flower essences energetically broadcast these qualities through all our relationships. The combination can be used in any situation where we need to feel this connection with our heart more strongly. In particular, it can be used as follows:

As **tonic and nourishment for the heart and emotions**.

To **soothe, comfort and warm the heart** when it feels cold and sad.

To **clarify the 'heart' of things**.

To help you **stay centred in love**.

To support you in **giving and receiving with greater joy and tenderness**.

To open you more deeply to the **beauty and treasures** within your own heart and the hearts of others.

To help you **radiate** your heart energy.

It is also possible to use Heart Balm at deeper levels and longer-term. It is a combination which helps to temper a relationship that is discordant, perhaps based on old misunderstandings or fears, and where resentments and unspoken feelings have distorted the natural grain of the relationship. The combination reminds us that every relationship is sacred and helps us to come back to a place of openness and curiosity where we are more able to discover its deeper spiritual significance. It helps to heal the heart's hurts and lift us to a more refined level of relating to others where our heart is open, trusting and adventurous enough to engage.

Heart Balm Mist enables us to use the combination at another level to create a loving and supportive ambience and to directly soothe our auric field and that of others. It can be misted around before a family gathering or celebration to help create an atmosphere of open-heartedness and mutual joy and appreciation. It can be used when you are staying in a strange place and want to relax and feel at home, especially when you go to sleep at night. You can also mist it around yourself when you are going through a time which feels troubling and painful to your heart. And it can be used in the home to help with peaceful and loving relationships between family members.

Heart Balm Mist contains: *Heart Balm Combination and organic essential oils of Mandarin, Rose Otto, Vanilla, Geranium and High Altitude Lavender.*

LIGHT SUPPORT COMBINATION

To help you connect with your inner light and strength during dark and difficult times

Light Support Combination contains a carefully blended selection of flower, gem and environmental essences which together help to bring support, clarity and insight during dark and difficult times. The combination helps to nurture your inner light and strength so that you are able to stay clear and heart-centred on your path, even in troubling and confusing situations. It assists you in finding your way through challenging circumstances in a more easeful and congruent manner.

Angel Star – helps us to stay connected with our inner guidance when we are beset by confusion and darkness, and when we feel swayed by the strong opinions of others about how best to proceed. Angel Star helps us to slip beneath this chaos and find our own truth waiting for us beneath, quietly and peacefully. It supports us in staying clear, defined and certain in the face of fears and uncertainties.

Golden Light – During times of darkness and challenge we can find ourselves going into despair, feeling that the future is bleak and our dreams are shattered. This essence helps us to lift our eyes beyond the situation we are in and take heart from the love and joy that will return on our path ahead. Acting as a balm for the spirit, it brings relief as we begin to feel our hope return and the way ahead become lighter and clearer.

Grass of Parnassus – Fear and trauma can cause us to leak our power and light away, at the very time when we most need them. Grass of Parnassus helps us to hold onto our strength and prevents it ebbing away. Along with Angel Star it keeps our crown chakra open so that we can stay aligned and in our power, able to respond as we need to.

Ruby-in-the-Storm – When trauma comes it can feel like our known world has suddenly become alien and unfamiliar. We can feel incredibly frightened, unsafe, rudderless and powerless. Ruby-in-the-Storm helps us to sit firmly in our heart – the peaceful centre at the eye of any storm – and find our courage and our love here to steady us through the most profound changes.

Scots Pine Sentinel – Feeling shaky, ungrounded and uncertain of where we are or what is our direction forward, we can lose contact with our inner compass that keeps us pointing to true Self and helps us navigate our way through the fog. Scots Pine Sentinel restores us to this inner connection, helping us to trust that our feet are still on the path, even though the route may be unfamiliar - and all shall be well. It brings the grounding and reassurance of the pine essences which help us to feel at home within.

This combination is deeply comforting and reassuring, as well as being empowering. When people take it they often comment first on how it touches the crown chakra in particular. This essence helps us to stay very grounded and earthed (with its powerful gem and tree essences) but also very strongly aligned with Spirit (with the two white star-like flower essences). It can be used in any situation where we need to feel this connection. In particular, it can be used as follows:

In any acute **shock and trauma**, from receiving bad news, being in or witnessing an accident, etc. - Light Support helps you **regain your centre, re-focus and reconnect with your inner calm.**

In **overwhelming emotional states** such as distress, panic, despair, sadness - to help you **ride the waves of the emotion and assist you in coming through**.

For situations where you require a **strong connection with your inner strength and to let your light shine** - standing up for your beliefs, speaking your truth, public speaking, exams - Light Support helps you **stay connected** with your courage and inner strength.

It is also possible to use Light Support at deeper levels, potentially longer-term. This would include working with: feelings of darkness and despair; loss of connection with your true self; integration of one's shadow; facing death; more congruent expression of self in the world; deeper connection with one's spiritual self; learning to stand strong, light and powerful in a balanced way.

Light Support Mist can be used to clear negative energy from a room or from a person's aura. It is used a lot by healers to clear the energy between consultations so that the room feels fresh and vibrant, and also to spray over a person when doing body-work to help release blocked or dark energy from their aura.

It can be sprayed in a car after any shock that might make you feel ungrounded and destabilized when you need to continue driving. It can also be used in the same way in any room of the house after an accident, thereby helping to restore a sense of safety and clarity once more.

Sprayed around a house or the boundaries of the garden and home, the essence can help release negativity and prevent the tendency to attract more of this. Once or twice a year I spray this around the house and garden with the intention of cleansing and protecting the space. I then use Heart Balm Mist to bring in loving and tender energies.

Light Support Mist contains: *Light Support Combination and organic essential oils of Lavender, Bergamot, Sage, Ravensara and Neroli.*

LOVING DESIRE COMBINATION

To support the loving expression of your sensual nature. To nurture tender and joyful physical intimacy.

Loving Desire Combination is a carefully blended selection of flower and gem essences to help nurture your sensual self and connect you more deeply with your physicality and sexuality in ways which are tender, joyful and loving. The combination supports you in finding your appropriate and individual expression of physical intimacy, in ways which support and uphold you and your beloved.

Aragonite – In order to feel comfortable with our sensual and sexual nature, we need to feel comfortable and at ease in our own body. Aragonite helps us to be fully embodied in a way which feels safe. It keeps us connected with ourselves as physical beings, and helps us to cherish our body and to relax any tension in our muscles and energy that prevent us from flowing with our physicality.

Chickweed Wintergreen – Sexuality suffers from many myths and loaded images in our society. For guilt and shame associated with sexuality, with past experiences, or with sexual fantasies, Chickweed Wintergreen helps restore our composure, balance and calm. It serves energetically to wipe the slate clean so that we are able to move forward feeling cleansed and open in our sexual union.

Dark Red Helleborine – The body contains incredible mysteries and gifts of which we may only know a few. With this essence we are able to connect more deeply with the wonders of our own body, from the simplest level of sensual enjoyment to harnessing and bathing in the energy of the kundalini. Dark Red Helleborine prompts us to discover and unlock the secrets of the body, gently and appropriately.

Pink Purslane – Loving intimacy is the heart of a beautiful sexual connection with our beloved. Pink Purslane guides us to open our heart to the daily intimacies of relating to our significant other – through touch, through words, through love-making, through the many ways in which we can express and delight in our contact with each other. It helps bring the relationship safely through the mundanity of everyday life, helping us to continually connect together joyously and creatively.

Venus Transit – We each have masculine and feminine sides, regardless of our sex. Venus Transit helps to balance these appropriately within us. The essence helps liberate and uphold the natural expression of our sensual and sexual nature and connect us with the spiritual Source of this. Along with Dark Red Helleborine it strengthens our awareness of the divine and the mystical in our sexual union.

Vernal Equinox – Where Aragonite supports us in feeling comfortable with our physical nature in general, Vernal Equinox enables us to embody our sacral chakra fully. This is an area that is blocked for many people. The essence helps restore flow and equilibrium here, gently returning us to our sacral power and vitality.

Our sexual energy is our life-force and our means of procreation so it is an incredibly powerful, emotive and potentially transcendent force. Learning to enjoy this, to harness it lovingly and pleasurably, and to have it be a healthy part of our life, is paramount for our health and wellbeing. This essence helps at each level – on the threshold of our sexuality or at any stage thereafter. It is gentle and easy to use. Many people choose to take it long-term where sexual issues run deep. The essence helps to regenerate and restore our connection with our sexuality to one which is divinely guided, beautiful to experience, and tender and vital in its expression. In particular, the combination can be used as follows:

To help you **express, explore, celebrate and experience the pleasure of your sensual/ sexual self.**

When you are experiencing difficulties **owning and expressing your sexuality** in ways which truly harmonise with your own sensual nature and that of your lover.

In the day-by-day unfolding of your relationship long-term, to help you **keep deepening your connection, trust and intimacy.**

To help **men connect with their masculinity and women with their femininity.**

To help **overcome fears, lack of interest, and alienation** from your sensual and sexual self.

To remind you to **embrace your sensual nature** when you are not in a sexual relationship.

It is also possible to use Loving Desire at a deeper level and longer-term to address long-standing difficulties of intimacy in a relationship, for lack of confidence or poor self-image regarding your body and sensuality, to help you discern and move away from a sexual union which is destructive to your wellbeing, or to help support feelings of safety and gentleness if you have had difficult sexual experiences in the past.

    Loving Desire Mist can be used to create an ambience that feels romantic, intimate and tender. Misting around your aura every morning and evening will support you in reaching towards a more sensual and tender awareness of your physicality. You may also want to spray it around your aura before or after love-making. It can be misted over your bed and around your bedroom every few days to nurture a loving environment.

Loving Desire Mist contains: *Loving Desire Combination and organic essential oils of Ylang Ylang, Grapefruit, Patchouli, Helichrysum, Rosemary.*

ANIMAL SUPPORT COMBINATION

To help create a loving bond between you and your animal. To help animals settle and feel at home in their environment and with each other.

Animal Support Combination is a selection of flower and gem essences for animals. It can be used regularly with pets to help create and support a loving bond between you and your animal(s), and to help animals feel at home in their environment and with each other. It helps to create feelings of safety and security and also brings accord to animals' relations with each other and with humans. For trauma you can combine this essence with Light Support to help an animal feel grounded and able to move through shock. To aid their healing process you can combine it with Healing Light. Where there is severe discord between animals or with animals and humans, use with Heart Balm.

Administering essences to animals: You can give essences to an animal by placing two or three drops on your hands and gently rubbing through their fur, morning and night. Alternatively, place two drops in a litre of water and put this in their water bowl so that they take it each time they drink. Replace daily. You can also use the misting spray – either your own, or the ready-made mist which includes essential oils. Do not spray this directly at the animal; instead lightly mist above their sleeping area, litter tray and/or eating area once or twice a day.

Grand Quintile – Animals need to know their own territory and the rules of their home so that they can feel safe and accepted in their home environment. Grand Quintile helps in establishing this without fear. At a deeper level it promotes trust and open-heartedness, and an inner sense of safety which does not require the animal to become aggressive, defensive or overly protective in its behaviour.

Grass of Parnassus – In situations where an animal feels insecure, perhaps through trauma or through bullying and intimidation from another animal or from a human, an animal can feel as worthless and frightened as we can. This essence helps an animal stay in its own personal power without it ebbing away.

Greater Cuckooflower – This essence supports community, friendship and heart-based relationships. It is important that there is love and accord between animals and humans who are going to be spending many years in each other's company. The essence promotes trust and fellow-feeling and brings a gentle sense of togetherness without creating a defensive or exclusive sense of a 'pack'.

Pink Purslane – Contact between animals and between animals and humans is often through touch. This essence supports touch that is appropriate, mutually joyful and tender. It helps animals to play well together and be more gentle in their physical contact with each other. It also helps humans who are too rough or invasive in the way they make physical contact with their animals.

Primrose – Animal relationships can be as imbalanced and one-sided as those of humans. This essence helps to re-establish good relations. It will help where one animal is more dominant than another, or where an animal or human is too dominant for the other. It will help where displays of affection are inappropriate, too intense or very distant. Primrose helps those in the relationship to come back to their point of balance so that all concerned feel much safer and happier once more.

Ruby-in-the-Storm – Animals can find their whole world change conclusively and without warning: this may be when they are taken from their mother to a new home; are left by their human family when they go on holiday, when their owner dies, etc. It can also be when they suffer from illness or an accident, or are abandoned, abused or neglected. Ruby-in-the-Storm helps an animal to regain its courage and its optimism when it faces frightening change and has become depressed or nervous.

This combination is gentle and soothing, helping the animal to connect with its inner strength and stability, come through transitions smoothly, and establish harmonious and trusting relationships. This combination helps your animal:

Feel **safe and supported during times of upset and upheaval** where it may feel disorientated and insecure.

When it is moving to a new home and needs to **adapt and find its feet again**.

When parted from you during holidays or other **periods of absence** where it may pine and fret.

When a **new animal is introduced** into the home to help establish good relations with humans and animals alike.

For animals who have **inharmonious relationships** with each other or with you.

Where animals have **suffered abuse and trauma in the past and find it difficult to trust and interact**.

It is also possible to use this essence deeper and longer-term to support relationships on a daily basis and to help humans and animals alike stay balanced and tender in their interactions with each other, coming to a level of interaction and accord which is intuitive and mutually uplifting.

Animal Support Mist can be used to create a protective, soothing space for your animal whenever you feel it needs additional support. Or use every few days to uplift and refresh the energy in its sleeping area, etc., so that it creates a light and energetically safe area for the animal to be in.

It is worth adding a note about Animal Support regarding those humans who have found themselves taking it for their own support (myself included)! This is a combination which helps to establish tranquillity, a feeling of settling and accord, and a pervasive sense of being reassured at some level. I have had several people suggest that this should also be called People Support because it is so calming and gentle! The spray, in particular, has a soft, fresh scent like a herb meadow in summer and it helps to invoke that same sense of relaxation and spaciousness we get when we lie in the grass in the sun. So this is just to assure you that all essences are for humans and animals alike, and you are not turning into your favourite pet if you find yourself reaching for this essence! Children, in particular, often intuitively select Animal Support when picking their own essences, and the mist has been known to help those who have difficulty sleeping to settle down more easily at night. I use the mist in my house, ostensibly for my animals, when I sense that things feel uneasy or unsettled in the environment and I want to restore a sense of peace and safety. But I have found it does me as much good as it does them!

Animal Support Mist contains: *Animal Support Combination and organic essential oils of Helichrysum, Sweet Fennel, Juniper, Lemon, Clary Sage and Palma Rosa.*

Part Four

Repertory

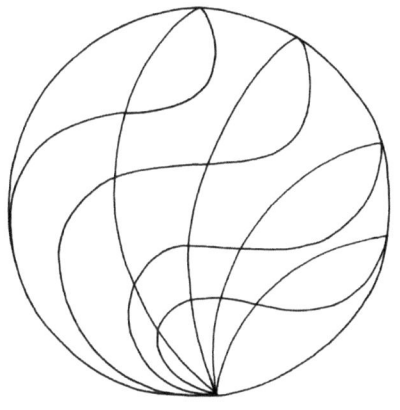

Repertory

The following themed areas give insights into appropriate essences for specific emotions, energetic states and situations. This can be used as an adjunct to intuitive prescribing, as a tool in its own right or as a means of finding the general 'ball-park' from which to select essences.

ABUNDANCE

Bountiful Life - reconnecting with that which is of true value in your life and attracting more of this.
Frog Orchid - opening to the flow of everyday miracles.
Golden Light - creating the life of your dreams; playful, light, joyous.
Hawthorn Blossom - fully receiving / appreciating the abundance you have.
Hawthorn Berries - fruition; harvest; fulfilling the true desires of your heart.

ALIGNMENT

Angel Star - aligning with your truth and inner voice; feeling more 'defined' and clear in who you are.
Balnakeil Bay - aligning with your true and deepest potential as a human being; self-realisation.
Hawthorn Berries - aligning with your deepest wishes / your heart's desires; bringing these into your life.
Healer's Light - aligning with your Healing; alignment of chakras and subtle energy bodies of aura.
Light Support - to align with your Self; to clear blocks to this; clearing and balancing the subtle energy in your space and aura.

ANGER

Fly Orchid - transmuting dark clots of consciousness; releasing available energy as a healing resource, a source of strength and wisdom (combine with *Silver Birch 'Fire'* and *Light Support* for deep anger).

Heart Balm - returning to the gentleness of the heart in times of anger.

Light Support - not reacting; staying aligned, self-contained, centred; able to respond.

Silver Birch 'Fire' - empowered; for walking in the realms of your most fiery emotions; harnessing these for peace.

Starry Saxifrage - balancing the ego with spirituality; comprehending the deeper issues; calming.

Twinflower - hearing the heart beneath the anger; deep listening to another's needs.

Venus Transit - understanding the necessity of letting things be disrupted / change /breakdown in order that something new can be born.

ANIMALS

Place a few drops of the essence on your hands and smooth through their fur.

Animal Support - for creating a safe, loving environment for animals; strengthening bond between animals and with carers; appropriate relating; to help bring calm and security.

Heart Balm – to support an animal during loss, grief or absence of loved ones when they are pining; to help with relationships that are discordant.

Light Support – for shock, trauma and distress.

Twinflower, Bogbean and Moonwort combined - to understand at a deep, subliminal level, the communication of another other than through words.

BODY

Aragonite - embracing your physicality; feeling secure in your body; releasing blocks to energy flow.

Butterfly Orchid - removing blocks to energetic flow and fluidity throughout whole body; alignment of flow.

Dark Red Helleborine - unlocking the secrets of your body; understanding its mysteries and potential.

Grand Quintile - releasing defensive energy patterns somatised in your body.

Herb Paris - supporting the structural integrity of the energetic and physical systems of the body.

Lady's Slipper Orchid – reconnecting with the movement and flow of your vital force and understanding how to live in accord with this.

Marsh Marigold - grounding excessive mental energy; balancing mind and body.

Moonwort - understanding the body's communications through symptoms / dreams at subconscious levels.

Self Heal - heeding and responding to the body's need for nurture.

Vernal Equinox - safe return to flow and creativity in the sacral chakra; healing after trauma here.

Aragonite, Pink Purslane and Self Heal combined - for lack of connection to and love of physical body; develops tender and intuitive connection.

BOUNDARIES

Angel Star - staying clear and defined within own energy; awareness of potential energy violation.

Grand Quintile - developing clear boundaries without fear and defensiveness.

Primrose - loving boundlessly whilst accepting the boundaries of relating.

Ring of Brodgar - feeling protected; held within a sacred space.

Silver Birch 'Fire' - creating a fire wall; for when boundaries are threatened.

CELEBRATION

Fragrant Orchid - harmonious connection with others; understanding the deeper significance of the group or gathering.

Frog Orchid - joyfully entering the flow of miracles.

Golden Light - invoking qualities of light, joy, play, dancing, spontaneity.

Greater Cuckooflower - fosters feelings of togetherness, social ease, community, communion.

Monkshood - for celebrating as a family or community, 'good medicine' – coming together in healing and love to strengthen bonds.

Ring of Brodgar - connecting with the sacred and celebratory; for ceremonies, rituals, rites of passage.

Scots Primrose - connecting with the deep treasures of the heart; meeting others with openness and joy.

Grandmother Pine, Lunar Standstill and Venus Transit combined - for women's celebrations/times together; coming together in feminine energy.

CHILDHOOD

Frog Orchid - open to miracles; joyous acceptance of this in one's life.

Golden Light - connecting with joy, spontaneity, play of childhood; confidence to dream, create and imagine.

Spring Squill - wiping the energetic slate clean after trauma in childhood; innocence, trust and hope.
Spring Squill and Chickweed Wintergreen - to aid healing after abuse in childhood.

DEATH AND DYING

Alpine Forget-Me-Not - connecting with Divine Love; knowing there is no loss or separation - only infinite Love.
Angel Star - guiding light; inner knowing; finding the luminous threads of truth to follow when the way seems dark and confusing.
Grand Quintile - knowing that we are all One; feeling the truth of this; surrendering to this.
Light Support - connecting deeply with your inner light and strength when facing the dark; support, safety, centring; finding your way to the Light.
Light Support Mist - spray around the room to aid transition to the Light.
Ruby-in-the-Storm - courage in the heart during major transition.
Scots Pine Sentinel - when feeling lost and afraid; finding one's inner compass and path again.
Scots Primrose - deep connection in heart with compassion, unconditional love and the heart's radiance; moving forward with love.
Spring Greens - creates a soothing healing environment in which to move forward; renewal, rebirth, new life.

FEMININE ENERGY

Grandmother Pine – reaching for the strength and knowing of our 'Grandmother wisdom' / our inner Elder and Matriarch; accessing qualities of nurturing, protection, authority and deep insight; balancing one's own needs and rhythms with those of the family/community.
Lunar Standstill - flowing with rhythms of moon and tide, of birth and change, of cycles of life; helpful to balance oneself within hormonal cycles.
Twinflower – balancing the masculine and feminine within; creating a loving discourse between these two aspects of your being; facilitating this ease in your external relationships.
Venus Transit – for deeply connecting with the Divine Feminine within and the powerful gifts this offers; learning to wield the potency of this awesome inheritance with strength and gentleness.
Greater Cuckooflower, Pink Purslane and *Spring Squill* – deeply relaxing into sensuality and play; reconnecting with the body, with expression, with Life through sensing and listening; feeling one's way forward.

FLOW

Aragonite - helps energy flow and circulate in your body; release of blocks.
Butterfly Orchid - flowering and alignment of subtle energy throughout your being.
Dark Red Helleborine - reveals key to release for stuck patterns/energy.
Grand Quintile - embracing and connecting with energetic flow of all life; not restricting/obstructing it.
Lunar Standstill - flowing with the energy of change; overcoming resistance; finding the wisdom in the change.
Marsh Marigold - freeing mental blocks due to overwork, fatigue, etc.; restores creativity and clarity.
Silver Birch 'Fire' - enables you to feel strong emotions in peaceful ways and let their energy flow.
Vernal Equinox - supports and increases healthy energetic flow in the sacral chakra.

FRUITION

Balnakeil Bay - fulfilling one's potential as a human being; self-realisation; fruition as an individual.
Bee Orchid - support in finding and bringing to fruition your life's work.
Bountiful Life - welcoming and receiving appropriate bounty.
Golden Light - creating the life you wish to live; bringing your dreams for the future to fruition.
Hawthorn Berries - fulfilling your heart's desires; receiving the fruits of your labour.
Spring Squill - for catching and holding onto one's childhood dreams; keeping one's sense of destiny intact; walking towards this.

GRIEF / LOSS

Alpine Willowherb - tending deeply held wounds in the heart; heart balm.
Bluebell - trust in Love again after hurt, betrayal, loss, pain; regenerating.
Ruby-in-the-Storm - staying centred in heart during turbulent times.
Scots Primrose - moving through grief to deeper gifts of the heart; deepening compassion.
Heart Balm Mist - for creating a soothing environment to support the heart.
Heart Balm *and* **Light Support** *combined or alternating* - for acute support during overwhelming emotion or deep introversion and shut-down.

GROUNDING

Aragonite - being fully grounded in your physicality; being more deeply embodied.

Grandfather Pine - reaching back to our ancestral roots, our male energy, being anchored by this.

Grandmother Pine - reaching back to our ancestral roots, our female energy, being anchored by this.

Light Support - connecting with your inner light and strength; feeling calm, certain, able to respond.

Scots Pine Sentinel - nurtures feelings of grounding and certainty when feeling lost and afraid.

GUIDANCE

Angel Star - connecting with inner guidance, self-awareness; following one's intuition.

Light Support - connecting with your inner light and being guided by this.

Marsh Felwort - heeding inner guide; applying your spiritual knowledge and wisdom practically.

Moonwort - de-coding the guidance of the subconscious through dreams, etc.

HEALTH

Butterfly Orchid - bringing in pure healing energy from Source for self and others; protection for healers against using up own energy supply.

Healer's Light - connecting with your own healing vitality and channelling this energy; moving beyond internal and external obstacles to healing; trust in the healing process.

Herb Paris - aligning with inherent structures of body and aura; connecting with pre-physical blueprint of health and re-establishing this in your body.

Lady's Slipper Orchid - recovering faith in your ability to heal; moving out of despair and loss of hope; reconnecting with inner wisdom and life-force.

Self Heal - understanding where your own health lies; reading the body's signs; returning to self-nurture and self-care.

Spring Greens - creating the internal and external energetic matrix to support wholeness and healing; tranquillity.

HEART

Alpine Willowherb - touching, tending, releasing deeply held wounds in the heart; allowing connection with heart so healing may gently flow there.

Bluebell - where the heart is shut down in negativity, suspicion, resentment; enables trust and openness to return; vulnerability and strength.

English Bearsfoot - cleanses and rejuvenates the heart's energy where there is a sense of negativity and darkness in the heart.

Heart Balm - to tend and support the heart's blossoming in every way.

Primrose - establishing and maintaining good relationships, heart-to-heart.

Ruby-in-the-Storm - staying centred in the heart during times of immense and potentially distressing change; remaining connected with your heart.

Scots Primrose - uncovering the depths and jewel of the heart; deeper qualities of compassion, forgiveness, unconditional love.

Twinflower - lovingly listening to your beloved; heeding their needs.

INDIVIDUALITY

Angel Star - feeling clear, defined and at one with who you are; knowing your own path as distinct from that of others.

Bee Orchid - manifesting your individual life's work, connecting with/ realising what you are here to do.

Grass of Parnassus - confidence to be who you are in all your beauty, not denying your essential nature.

La Meije - heeding your path and calling in life; following your individual spiritual path and destiny.

INNOCENCE

Bluebell - return to an innocent belief in love /relationships after trauma; wisdom of experience.

Chickweed Wintergreen - return to innocence after experiences that have brought shame and guilt.

Spring Squill - childhood innocence; restoring peace and innocence where blighted by a frightening or restrictive childhood.

LIFE'S WORK

Bee Orchid - support and confidence to create and bring to manifestation your own life's work; holds the template for what is being created.

La Meije - to inspire and hold you steady when facing your path and calling.

Marsh Felwort - applying your inner wisdom practically to support your life's work; discipline and resolve.

LIGHT AND DARK

Angel Star - guiding light; inner knowing; finding the luminous threads of Truth to follow when the way is dark and confusing.

Chickweed Wintergreen - absolution from feeling energetically tainted or shamed by dark experiences.

English Bearsfoot - restoring luminosity and radiance to the dark heart.

Fly Orchid - transmuting dark clots of consciousness; finding the gifts in dark times.

Grass of Parnassus - staying powerful in your light; not leaking your power and light away; being comfortable with your light and purity.

Light Support - connecting deeply with your inner light and strength during dark times; support, safety, centring.

LOVE

Alpine Forget-Me-Not - connecting with Divine Love as a real presence.

Alpine Willowherb - balm for heart's pain; moving on from wounds; letting your heart's softness gently radiate out again.

Bluebell - restoring trust in Love after experiences of loss, betrayal or abandonment; open to loving again; mature and compassionate love.

English Bearsfoot - renewing, regenerating, cleansing the heart to love in clean, untainted ways.

Grand Quintile - moving beyond states of separateness, defensiveness, difference; knowing and living your Oneness.

Heart Balm - to tend and support the heart's blossoming in every way.

Loving Desire - loving sensual and sexual connection with your beloved.

Primrose - good love; giving and receiving appropriate expressions of love

Scots Primrose - opening to deeper levels of loving communion with others; unconditional love; compassion; forgiveness.

MASCULINE ENERGY

Bogbean - bringing sensitivity and awareness where there is overly combative/unsympathetic Yang energy.

Grandfather Pine - appropriate, dynamic expression of male energy; wisdom; grounding; maturity in word and deed.

Scots Pine Sentinel - certainty, clarity of action, strong internal sense of direction, ability to lead responsibly.

Silver Birch 'Fire' - harnessing and expressing yang energies peacefully and authoritatively; not being overwhelmed by passionate and fiery energies.

Twinflower – balancing the masculine and feminine within; creating a loving discourse between these two aspects of our being; facilitating this ease in our external relationships.

Venus Transit - profound balancing of masculine and feminine energies.

MATURITY

Bluebell - Maturing expression of love; moving beyond the demands of unreal expectations and idealism to acceptance and joy.

Cobweb Houseleek - finding new depths of maturity/endurance during difficult or 'lean' times.

Globeflower - moving beyond seeing one's own needs to seeing the needs of all; interdependence.

Grandfather Pine - wisdom of experience; ability to discern; supporting others with paternal guidance and care; true wisdom.

Grand Quintile - maturity in consciousness: living with deep awareness of the Oneness of all things.

MEDITATION

Alpine Aster - reconnecting with inner haven, spiritual blueprint; coming back to who you are and why you are here.

Alpine Forget-Me-Not - connecting with Divine and Universal Love.

Le Jardin Des Alpes - coming to a peaceful, restful place within (combine with Alpine Aster to make a meditation-space essence mist).

Light Support Mist - assists meditation by bringing light, clarity and alignment to the energy of your space/your subtle energy pathways.

Marsh Felwort - discipline to establish a regular practice and heed and live by the insights that come.

Serenity - returning to the inner peace behind the external drama; support in stepping up to a new level of consciousness.

MIND

Angel Star - finding your way through confusing thoughts and doubts; restoring inner certainty and calm.

Light Support - releasing tangled, dark thoughts; shining a clear light into the mind; restoring mental and emotional equilibrium.

Marsh Marigold - restores clarity and acuity to the mind after over-work or if

you are too much in the head.
Serenity - moving from one level of consciousness to the next; releasing old patterns of thinking.

ONENESS

Alpine Aster - restoring inner communion with one's wholeness.
Globeflower - understanding the inter connectedness of all things; having responsibility for one's place and part in the whole; ripple-effect.
Grand Quintile - moving beyond concepts of separateness and difference to understanding we are all One.
One-Flowered Wintergreen - deeply sensing and receiving the Good in All.
Ring of Brodgar - oneness with the Earth; connection with the sacred forces of Nature; connection with humanity through Nature.
Scots Primrose - opening one's heart to Oneness; embracing, accepting and meeting all with love and deep trust as part of the Everything.

PERSPECTIVE

Bird's Eye Primrose - seeing truly; clear and vital inner vision; ability to hold the inconsistencies of internal and external reality and see clearly.
La Meije - seeing beyond our fears when facing our true path and calling.
Monkshood - viewing things from the perspective of community; seeing what is for the good of all.

PLAY

Golden Light - invigorating light, happiness, play; to reconnect with your dreams; to re-imagine your future full of bright colours, laughter and love.
Le Jardin Des Alpes - taking time to rest, renew, play, recharge, away from the busyness and bustle of life; feeling too serious and weighed down.
Spring Squill - restoring a sense of innocence, play, delight, joy; reconnecting with your inner child.

POWER

Angel Star - clearly perceiving where others may be manipulating you; returning to own clarity, independence, individual voice.
Grand Quintile - moving away from defensiveness to clear boundaries and to love; secure in own connection with unconditional love; not threatened.
Grass of Parnassus - standing in one's power without feeling embarrassed or

arrogant; humble acceptance of your own gifts; not leaking power away.
Light Support - reconnecting with your inner light, strength and power.
Silver Birch 'Fire' - harnessing your fiery emotions powerfully for peace.
Starry Saxifrage - moving beyond ego-driven ambition; spiritual power.

PROTECTION

Grand Quintile - helping one to move beyond defensiveness when feeling
under threat, to having clear and loving boundaries.
Heart Balm - coming from a place of love and nurture; returning to your
heart, open and unafraid; trust in what Is.
Light Support - protection from manipulation by others or from dark
energies and confusing times (spray around home or as drops).
Ring of Brodgar - brings containment, safety; holding a sacred space in which
to be.

PROTECTION AGAINST ILLNESS

Healer's Light - take internally with either or both of the mists below being
used externally. This will help you stay connected with your healing needs
and vitality if you feel run-down or particularly susceptible to illness.
Healer's Light Mist - use to strengthen your aura against illness and to bring
clean, clear healing energy to your workspace/bedroom/home.
Light Support Mist – use the mist to spray around the outer edges of your
home/workspace/aura to clear negativity and stuck energy.

PURIFYING / CLEANSING

Butterfly Orchid - cleanse, align and restore flow of energy channels.
Chickweed Wintergreen - absolution; energetic cleansing, healing and renewal
where there has been shame and guilt.
English Bearsfoot - cleanses the heart of negativity; to remove all taint and
darkness from the heart.
Golden Light - restoration of child-like innocence; ability to look forward to a
bright future and re-create a more joyous past through future deeds.
Light Support - (especially **Light Support Mist**) cleanses and purifies;
removes stale, dark or stagnant energy from the aura or environment; protects,
cleanses, lightens.
Scots Primrose - to cleanse and polish the jewel of the heart.
Spring Squill - wiping the energetic slate clean after trauma in childhood;

innocence, trust and hope.

RELATIONSHIPS

Alpine Willowherb - tending the heart's wounds; moving beyond hurt into healing; supporting your heart while softly radiating out to others.

Angel Star - staying clear, light and defined on your own path when feeling pulled by the demands and needs of others.

Bluebell - trusting in love again after fear, distrust, betrayal, loss.

Fragrant Orchid - group harmony; understanding higher reason for being together as a couple/family/group/community.

Globeflower - knowing that we are all inter-related, 'what you do affects me'; responsibility for your place and part in the whole.

Grand Quintile - dissolving defences; moving beyond separateness to oneness.

Grass of Parnassus - feeling safe in own power and beauty; safe enough to shine your light without threatening or undermining others.

Greater Cuckooflower - forging strong bonds of friendship and trust.

Hawthorn Blossom - ceasing to yearn for what is not / believing 'the grass is greener elsewhere'; understanding the rich gifts and potential of your life now.

Heart Balm - to soothe, support and balance relationships; encourages warmth, compassion and intimacy; forgiveness and resolution.

Loving Desire - healthy, loving, sexual/sensual relationship.

Pink Purslane - supports long-term physical intimacy and commitment.

Primrose - creating good boundaries in relationships.

Silver Birch 'fire' - being with your fiery energies – anger, passion – in ways which are healthy and do not destroy your relationship.

Twinflower - tender listening to another's needs; subliminal level of listening.

Viper's Bugloss - learning to speak with love, care and truthfulness.

RENEWAL / RECHARGING

Alpine Aster - coming back to your spiritual blueprint, reconnecting deeply with who you are and why you are here.

Herb Paris - restoring and strengthening your inner sense of order, function, physical grounding, alignment.

Le Jardin Des Alpes - time out from busyness; rest, renewal, relaxation.

Silver Light - patiently attending change; surrendering to quiet times.

RETREAT

See RENEWAL/RECHARGING and also:

Dark Red Helleborine - reconnection with deep mystery and sacredness of life; regrouping to find key to release and to move forward.

Marsh Helleborine - confidence and inner security to move out into the world once more after being in retreat.

Moonwort - immersion in unconscious to discover meaning of dreams, symptoms, intuition; (combine with *Butterfly Orchid* and *Dark Red Helleborine* for deep Shamanic work to receive clear guidance).

Serenity - meditation, mindfulness; reaching the next level of consciousness.

SELF-REALISATION

Balnakeil Bay - realisation and fulfilment of your true nature.

Bee Orchid - manifesting the work you were born to do.

Dark Red Helleborine - uncovering latent knowledge and skills within yourself.

SENSUALITY AND SEXUALITY

Chickweed Wintergreen - where shame and guilt prevent one from enjoying one's sexual and sensual nature.

Dark Red Helleborine - uncovering the deep mysteries of one's sensual self; kundalini; spiritual and sexual balance.

Greater Cuckooflower - loving intimacy, connecting with another.

Loving Desire - to support and enable healthy, loving sexuality.

Pink Purslane - long-term commitment and deepening intimacy; sexual fidelity and accord with one's beloved.

Twinflower - sensing other's needs with care and attention; deep listening leading to deep communication of body and being.

Vernal Equinox - releases blocks and enables flow in sacral chakra; return to ease within the water element of your being.

SPEAKING

Light Support - strength and support in speaking your truth; letting your light shine when public speaking; courage to speak true.

Twinflower - moving beyond misunderstanding and misinterpretation in one-to-one relationships; hearing the other's needs and clearly voicing your own.

Viper's Bugloss - learning to use words to heal not harm; restoring own sacred discourse.

SPIRITUALITY

Alpine Forget-Me-Not - knowing as reality the Divine Love that surrounds and protects you; moving beyond this as a concept to the truth you live.
Butterfly Orchid - opening the channels of your energy bodies to the pure healing light of Spirit, for yourself and others.
La Meije - embracing your spiritual path and calling.
Marsh Felwort - spiritual discipline and resolve; practically applying and living the teachings of your spiritual self.
One-Flowered Wintergreen - receiving from the Benevolent Universe; seeing the good in all things.
Ring of Brodgar - sacred ceremony; rites of passage; affirmation of the sacred in your life.
Serenity - assists you in reaching the next level of consciousness; mindfulness, meditation.

STRENGTH

Cobweb Houseleek - plumbing profound inner depths of resourcefulness and strength during lean times.
Light Support - connecting with your inner light and strength, especially in times of difficulty and darkness.
Monkshood - recognising and drawing to you that which strengthens you and your community; finding your 'good medicine' and embracing this.
Ruby-in-the-Storm - staying centred in the heart, loving and compassionate, in the eye of the storm.

SUPPORT

Bee Orchid - manifesting your life's work when it feels there is no external support or encouragement; spiritual support; creative inspiration.
Cobweb Houseleek - finding within yourself deep internal resources and endurance during lean times.
Grandfather Pine - support of ancestral wisdom; 'grandfather wisdom'.
Grandmother Pine - support of ancestral wisdom; 'grandmother wisdom'.
Grand Quintile, Marsh Helleborine and *Greater Cuckooflower* - reaching out to others for support; moving beyond defensiveness; network of friendship, care and solidarity.
Heart Balm - supports, deeply tends, soothes and brings healing to the heart.
Light Support - for connecting with your inner light and strength during dark and difficult times.
Ruby-in-the-Storm - staying centred in your heart during times of change and

disorientation; knowing your heart is a worthy vessel in the toughest storms.

TRUST

Alpine Forget-Me-Not - knowing you are divinely loved and are safe.
Angel Star - trusting your inner voice and guidance.
Bee Orchid - self-worth in your work; trust that you can manifest this.
Bluebell - trusting in love; having the courage to love again, deeply.
La Meije - trusting the path that opens before you; knowing you are guided by Spirit; having courage to reach beyond your comfort zone into the new.
Marsh Helleborine - trusting that you are ready to move out into the world.
Pink Purslane - trust in physical intimacy and long-term commitment.

VISION

Angel Star - offers a tiny thread of gold to follow in very dark times; reconnecting with your truth, your way.
Bee Orchid - manifesting the vision of your work in this world.
Bird's Eye Primrose - inner vision; clarifying your ability to see true; regaining perspective, being able to look around and see all ways.
La Meije - heeding the vision of your path and calling; courage to meet this.
Silver Birch 'fire' - reconnecting with the visionary aspect of yourself; being wise enough and quick enough to see; harnessing your fiery element.

VITALITY

Aragonite - reconnection with your physical body as your spirit's home; supporting it with reverence and respect; becoming re-embodied.
Cobweb Houseleek - supports you in finding deep levels of resourcefulness and endurance during lean times when there is little support or relief.
Healer's Light - reconnecting with our inner healer; assimilating higher levels of healing and vitality within our being.
Lady's Slipper Orchid - reconnecting with inner vitality and potency; healing potential.
Marsh Marigold - returning to the body after intense periods of work, study, etc., which have led to mental and physical fatigue.
Monkshood - recognizing that which is 'good medicine' for you in life, which supports, upholds and sustains you.
Vernal Equinox - restoring vitality and equilibrium to the sacral chakra; reconnecting with the water of life within yourself.

WAITING

Alpine Aster - taking time to reconnect with your spiritual blueprint, take stock, review your life direction; deep inner communion.

Le Jardin Des Alpes - inner contemplation, renewal, relaxation, meditation; time to be rather than do.

Silver Light - patiently attending the changes happening beneath the surface; poised and ready to act when the right time comes; no longer pushing.

WISDOM

Dark Red Helleborine - for attuning to the deep wisdom of the body.

Marsh Felwort - hearing and heeding your inner spiritual wisdom.

Marsh Marigold - understanding the difference between mental knowledge and deeper wisdom.

Appendix: Essence Making Methodologies

PLEASE NOTE: Only two of the LightBringer Essences described in this book have been made by cutting the blossoms from the plant – 'Angel Star' and the rose used in 'Venus Transit'. No other flowers have been cut or harmed to make these essences.

The information given below for Bach's original methodology cannot be used for rare flowers, such as those used in the LightBringer Essences. Please do not attempt to make your own essences from such plants. Flowers which are officially listed as endangered are in a critical condition and need to be given every opportunity to grow. It is illegal to take the blooms or otherwise interfere with such flowers without appropriate consent and supervision from the relevant authorities.

Please also be aware that many plants are poisonous to touch, cut and ingest as a tincture. Please check before making an essence. If in doubt, consult a good plant guide and contact the British Association of Flower Essence Producers for further information (see address details at the end of this section).

DR BACH'S METHODOLOGIES FOR MAKING ESSENCES

The following passage is extracted from Julian Barnard's book *The Healing Herbs of Edward Bach* with his kind permission. It gives a thorough explanation of the original methodology for making essences which Dr Bach set down and which Julian Barnard has gone on to use for the Healing Herbs essences (www.healingherbs.co.uk). This methodology has since been developed in many different ways by producers all over the world in the time since the 1920's when these directions culminated in the 38 Bach Flower Remedies.

PREPARING FLOWER ESSENCES

When Dr Bach set out to make an essence he prepared himself beforehand so that he was in a receptive and harmonious state. Then he was able to work with the healing forces of nature that were to be brought into focus in the remedy. He would take a bath, wear clean clothes, a white gown and, so we might guess, he also prepared himself mentally by a form of meditation. Making a flower remedy calls for our best endeavour in all respects whatever way we choose to approach the process for ourselves. The more we strive to understand what is involved the better we shall be able to see what exactly is appropriate. Having found, on a previous occasion, a place where the plants or trees grow particularly well, we should choose a fine day for making the remedy and have everything ready. We may need ladders for the trees if the flowers are out of reach or a walking stick to hook a branch. Secateurs and scissors may be required or another chosen cutting implement. We may need permission from the landowner. Whether the remedy is made by the sun method or whether it is a 'boiler', the jugs, bottles, water and brandy must all be prepared before we start.

The Flowers – It is important to choose a location where these are growing naturally. Whenever possible they should be in the wild, in a place where they are not interfered with by animals or people, and where the earth forces are strong and unpolluted by motorways, power stations and the like. It is apparent that many of the remedy trees and plants no longer grow in the same clear and healthy conditions that existed in Bach's time. There are physical and metaphysical forces that have weakened and distorted the land and the flowers. Where the natural balance has been maintained there the remedy will be strongest. With those trees and shrubs that are likely to have been planted, such as Red Chestnut, Walnut or Cerato we can find a place where the estate, farm or garden is sensitively cared for. When preparing a remedy use only those flowers that are in perfect bloom and select from several different plants or trees at the same location. Make doubly sure that this is the correct flower.

Equipment – A jug and funnel will be needed, the glass bowl or saucepan (according to which method is being used) and a bottle for storing the essence. These all need to be completely clean. They should be sterilised by boiling for twenty minutes in a large saucepan, wiped dry and wrapped in a clean cloth. A bottle of the purest water available is required (not distilled water) and a quantity of pure brandy to preserve the essence. Filter papers will be needed to strain the essences prepared by boiling.

Sun Method – Start making the essence before nine o'clock in the morning on a clear, bright, sunny day when there are no clouds in the sky. Take a thick glass bowl about 300ml or half pint size (not the oven-proof type) and fill it with pure water, preferably from a local spring. Pick the blooms from the plant and float them immediately on to the water. It may help if someone holds the bowl beneath the flower stems; alternatively carry the flowers on a broad leaf to avoid any contact with the hand. Cover the surface of the bowl and then top up the water if necessary. Leave it in the sunshine alongside the remedy plants for three to four hours, or less if the blooms show signs of fading. If the sun becomes clouded during this time the remedy should be abandoned. Avoid letting shadows fall across the bowl, whether your own or from plants and grasses. When they have given up their healing strength the flowers should be lifted out from the bowl using a twig of the plant rather than fingers. The essence is then poured into a clean, empty bottle so that an equal volume of brandy may be added as a preservative. It may be easier to use the brandy bottle itself since it should be sterile, mixing the brandy half and half with the essence. It is up to you how much essence you choose to keep. When the remedy has been prepared you will sense the vitality and see that the water has been subtly changed.

Boiling Method – Make the remedy on a bright day, picking the flowers before nine o'clock in the morning. Take a clean enamel saucepan (aluminium should be avoided, stainless steel could be used but enamel is best), and three-quarters fill it with the flowers and stems. These need to be about 15cm long depending on the width of the pan. Put the lid on and take the saucepan home without delay. Then cover the flowers and twigs with two pints (1.13 litres) of pure water and put the saucepan on to boil, without the lid on. Simmer for thirty minutes using a twig of the plant to press the contents down if necessary. When the time is up, replace the lid and put the pan outside to cool. When it is cold the essence should be filtered. It may be helpful to remove the twigs first, again using a piece of the plant and not fingers. After filtering pour the essences into a bottle half and half with brandy. The boiling method prepares a large volume of essence and not all of it need be kept. It is interesting to taste a glassful on its own. The saucepan must be thoroughly cleaned and then boiled, along with the other utensils, and stored for future use.

Essence: Stock: Medicine – When the essence is prepared and bottled it should be labelled. Provided it is kept free from physical and metaphysical interference it will retain its potency. Stock may be prepared by putting two drops of essence into a small (30ml) bottle filled with pure brandy. From such stock a chosen combination of remedies may be made up to medicine strength by placing two drops of each stock into a small bottle of water and brandy.

Dosage is then four drops of this four times a day. Alternatively the two drops of stock may be put into a glass of water and sipped.

THE LIGHTBRINGER ESSENCE METHODOLOGIES

The LightBringer Essences are made using certain key aspects of Dr Bach's sun methodology in terms of his care and mindfulness in preparing for and working with the flowers. However they are not made in the same way (see main part of the book for further details) but use a combination of several methodologies which have developed over time and which depend on where and how the plant grows. All the LightBringer Essences are what are called 'Living Essences' because the flower remains on the plant and is not cut so that it expends its life-force in the bowl. This is not better or worse than Dr Bach's methodologies; it simply offers another way of working with the subtle energy of plants and the result is a different kind of healing vibration. It also enables me to work with rare and poisonous plants without harm to them or myself. There are three main methodologies which I have listed below in the order in which I most commonly use them:

1.   Placing a bowl beside a flower so that it can hang into it. Its petals are touching the water but it is not cut.
2.   Suspending a bowl over a flower so that its inhalation and expiration is caught in the bowl as condensation and this drips down into a small bowl beneath for collection – lovely for small flowers growing near to the ground.
3.   Lightly sprinkling water through the flowers and catching this in a bowl below. The same water may be taken through the flowers several times. When using this method I particularly try to use water from a spring nearby.

The mother tincture is made as in Bach's methodology – half vodka and half the mother essence. A daughter essence is then made which refines the process further and creates a lighter essence – this seems to suit the very spiritual nature of the LightBringer Essences.

The stock essence is made by placing 5 drops of daughter essence in a 15ml bottle containing 40% water and 60% brandy. Making up the daughter essence and its first stock essence is a process of sacred ceremony and attunement, the directions for which came to me through a dream and shamanic journeys. It serves to welcome the healing properties of the plant / gem / environment into that essence, and to ask that it be consolidated, strengthened, blessed and made ready to go out into the world to give the gift of its healing in whatever way is appropriate for the person needing it. It is a very mindful process which involves connecting deeply with the subject and the mother essence together until a final charge is felt to enter the essence and it becomes a 'LightBringer' essence.

For further information regarding the making of essences and regulations for producers in the UK, please contact BAFEP:

British Association of Flower Essence Producers (BAFEP)

PO Box 100, Exminster, EXETER, Devon, EX6 8YT
Tel: 01392 832005
Website: www.bafep.com
Email: info@bafep.com

Acknowledgements

Making the LightBringer Essences is an act of co-creation. The journey to find them, understand them, realise them and imbibe them has been and continues to be one of profound grace. I feel delight and gratitude for this journey of Spirit and Nature.

I wish to thank most deeply and with love, the flower essence and healing community that I am privileged to be part of. In particular to Beth Tyers, whose art was in planting this seed for so many of us; Dave Evans who was my first homeopath and a generous and profound support; and Paul Francis who taught me the extent of the healing arts and held a space for me to explore and grow which was utterly beautiful, affirming and safe. Thank you to Ian Watson whose teachings and flower essence retreats ignited flames of inspiration and empowerment which have continued to fan my spirit and burn brightly - you are a source I keep returning to. Thank you to my students and clients with whom I have had the most humbling and amazing experiences and who ask the right questions to keep me journeying. Especial thanks to Vicky Peet and Laura Howie who have kindly looked after our home and our beloved Collie and Maine Coon when we have needed to journey to Scotland to make the next essences!

I would like to thank Ben, Sarah and Emily Tyers who have entrusted me with their mother's wonderful essence, Linden Blossom.

I thank Anne Waters, Phil May, Eliza Forder, Jill White, Daniel Mapel and Paul Lambeth – each of whom have taught me healing modalities of profound relevance – thank you for your wonderful and timely support. To Helen Bebbington in particular, sincere thanks go to you for your exquisite support in helping fine-tune the essence mists. Your knowledge in essential oils and their spiritual qualities is incredibly inspiring and I deeply appreciate the integrity with which you have approached this work.

I would like to thank Maggie Dudley and John Cameron for practical and insightful support which launched me in the early days and gave me much of the structure I have then been able to build on.

I thank Terri and Jim Hayes-Wallace who have provided such kind and sensitive support which has kept me going at times when I doubted I could do this.

I wish to thank Angie Jackson and Adam Rubenstein for the gift of exciting work over many years through Healthlines, for being fellow travellers on the essence road, and for the shared explorations we have in conversations, through our work and through our love of essences.

I thank Debbie Binch who, more than anyone I know, puts the environment first and has taught me to understand practically and pragmatically how we can be stewards of this wild and beautiful earth, and move towards a permaculture which – as the name suggests – enables the earth as we know and love it to be sustained.

I thank Jackie Stewart who has stepped in near the completion of this book, to bring her graceful energy to bear on its overall design and presentation, making it print-ready. It is a privilege to have your light touch and your flower-like energy on this project.

I wish to thank my dear friend, Muriel Pichard. Essences are a huge part of both our lives and of our journey together, giving us amazing support and understanding. I am grateful that you have been beside me through so many twists and turns of fortune and fate. It is deeply comforting to have such a friend to walk with.

I thank my dear friends Steve and Sue Craven whom I have known since I started secondary school, as a wobbly young thing with a passion for words. Thank you for the faith you have in me and the loving support and friendship you give. I cherish it and feel blessed to know you.

I thank Joan and Derek Singleton who have inspired me with their own beautiful books, their love and knowledge of the world outside the window, of timeless landscapes and the solace they can bring. Thank you for your support and love.

I thank Alessandro Riva, Monica Franceschini and Anna Liberti in Italy who have all worked so hard to translate the essence information and spread the word about the essences abroad with sensitivity and love. Thank you to Ale for knowing the essences almost as well as me and placing them so firmly in your heart. Thank you also to Salvatore Cali for the beautiful cosmogram that illustrates the chapters. It is very special to have this blending of our work, inspired by a love of Nature.

I thank John Williams whose intellect, encouragement, grammatical know-how, and above all, love, has sustained me and uplifted me. You have given me some literary tram-lines to walk down and provided me with a gentle stream of feedback which I have drawn much learning from. That the book is complete is testimony to the fact that my courage was fanned by your belief that I could absolutely do this. Our talks on abundance, music, literature and life, and our enjoyable lunches, have been wonderful punctuation along the way.

I thank my family – Philip for seeing in me a woman who could create her own niche and career, before I even knew this myself; David for your gift with language which is an incomprehensibly eloquent bench mark I test myself against, and for the searching questions you have posed to me about healing; Mary for the sweetness of spiritual recognition and understanding which we meet in each other and gain mutual comfort from; and John for knowing that all Addymans are capable of writing books, though I don't think the rest of us put together will produce as prolifically as you!

And I thank Marie who has brought me up with rare and healing plants ever-present and an incredible storehouse of knowledge regarding them; who has passed on to me a deep and abiding love of literature and of the power of words to shape things; and who has shown me the value of human creations beautifully made which has given me the courage to dare to create for myself. Thank you deeply for your love, courage and support.

And finally, with love, gratitude and joy, and from my heart, I thank my beautiful Bryan for the journey we are on and the richness this brings to my life. Words don't go there, my love.

And to the many others I have not been able to mention here who have been instrumental in supporting me on this journey, I give my grateful thanks.

CONTACT DETAILS

LIGHTBRINGER ESSENCES

To find out more about LightBringer Essences, to sign up for the newsletter, for information on workshops and for purchases through the on-line store, please contact us as follows:

Website:
www.lightbe.co.uk

Email:
admin@lightbe.co.uk

Telephone Number and Postal Address:
Please check the website for up-to-date information on our telephone number and postal address.

Please contact the author, Rachel Singleton, using the above details, if you would like to share information regarding your experiences of taking the LightBringer Essences. It is a great help to our ongoing research to receive your feedback.

LaVergne, TN USA
07 March 2011
2200LVUK00001B